Crystal Lea Essex

Fruitful

By Crystal Lea Essex

©2024 Crystal Lea Essex

Published by Purpose Media Publishing, Little Rock, AR

All rights reserved. No part of this publication may be reproduced, stored in a retrieval system, or transmitted in any form or by any means without the prior written permission of the publisher. The only exception is brief quotations in printed reviews.

ISBN: 979-8-8843692-0-7

For information, contact:
Purpose Media Publishing
P.O. Box 15561
Little Rock, AR 72231

Crystal Lea Essex
E-mail: Fruitful.thebook@gmail.com

Cover design: Faith Fernandez

Printed in the United States of America

For the one who's been *waiting*...

This is for you.

TABLE OF CONTENTS

Preface	9
Acknowledgements	11
Introduction	13
God Said It Was Very Good	17
Finding Light in a Dark Place	27
An Echoed Promise	33
It May Be	41
Passionate Desire	51
A Willingness to do Anything	59
Seeking His Truth	65
Thou Shall Conceive a Son	75
A Documented Miracle	81
Entering Into the Secret Place	95
The God Who Remembers Me	101
It Shall Be Well	107
A New Day is Dawning	117
I Will Do a New Thing	123
On the Other Side of Surrender	133
A Place of Rest and Safety	143
My Heart Doth Magnify the Lord	151
About the Authors	155

Preface

This book has been a burden on my heart since I first learned the healing power of Jesus is available to whosoever will believe in Him and walk according to His will. My husband and I have endured a season of infertility lasting more than 14 years, and in the darkest moments of this season, it was difficult to find resources for women who are on a similar journey and solely relying on the promises of God for strength. Most of the resources I've encountered speak of success after years of infertility only after treatment options involving infertility medication, surgical procedures, or adoption. While I don't want to discredit those avenues, deep in my heart I knew there had to be another option. What I didn't know was that option was on the other side of complete surrender, and what a beautiful journey it would be as the Creator of my body, the One who formed it in His hands, walked alongside me showing me that He was still the God who parted the waters and calmed the seas.

With estimations that nearly one in six women struggle with infertility, the purpose for this book is to put a resource in the hands of women who are looking for encouragement and a rekindled fire of hope and faith in the all-sustaining power of God to carry them along the way. Over the years, I have seen countless women struggle with choices that were heavy and hard to bear in their efforts to conceive. This journey is not for the faint of heart. I've seen women pressured into in vitro fertilization (IVF), even when they could not afford it, and the probability of a positive outcome was very low. Yet in their desperation, they agreed, as it seemed like their *only* option. For some, it was their last chance, their only chance. There is such an urgency in this hour for a reigniting of faith in divine intervention and the miracle-working power of our Almighty God.

Whether you are experiencing infertility, another seemingly insurmountable trial of life, or are ministering to those who face circumstances that require a greater measure of faith, it is my prayer that your faith in Him is increased as you turn through the pages of this book.

May God bless you and keep you!

Acknowledgements

Jesus, the true author of this story: Thank you for pulling me out of the darkness and into Your marvelous light. Thank you for being my Shepherd and leading me by the still waters and restoring my soul. For being my refuge and strength. For carrying my burdens when I couldn't. For sustaining and leading me on this beautiful journey.

Joey: I love you so much! You never gave up on me. Ever. I'm thankful God gave me you. Thank you for allowing me to sit for endless amounts of time while writing, and listening to my rants when I was hitting a brick wall. More importantly, thank you for being a big part of my story. I'm sorry you had to navigate this with me, but I couldn't think of anyone else I'd want to do life with. I love you!

Pastor Gordon Parrish: Thank you for being a godly example in my life, for shepherding me, and helping me to grow. Thank you for cheering me on along the way to this book. Your encouragement gave me great momentum. Thank you for believing in me.

Johnnie Dartt, Holly Bartlett, Kym Miller, and Cynthia Edmonds: Thank you for not only being such godly examples of holy women in my life, but for being my mentor and friends. I would not be the woman I am today without your influence. Thank you for your times of prayer and fasting that were directed toward me. I know God honored your prayers!

Kara Glodowski, Kristin Ikerd, Courtney Moncrief, Faith Fernandes, Jornie Kinga, Kathleen Steinhauer: Thank you for being such great friends, for always being encouraging, and for believing in me. More importantly, thank you for being there when I felt completely lost in grief. I don't know what I would have done without you.

Sis. Candy Saylor: You know me perhaps more intimately than anyone, except for Jesus. Thank you for walking through some of the darkest moments of my life with me unashamedly, leading me back to my Anchor and guiding me through inner healing so that I could have the strength move past my grief and actually finish this book. You are an angel sent by the Lord in my time of greatest need.

To my parents: Henry and Tresa Whetzel: Thank you for being there for me in my journey when I had no one else, for bearing my grief and my pain, and for loving me through this in a way that only parents can. I love you both very much!

Pat Cornwall (Mama Pat): Thank you for not taking no for an answer and for never forgetting to remind me of God's promises. You believed when it was hard for me to believe. Thank you!

Cindy Stageman, Daisy Edwards, Bobbie Hunter, Sarah Federline: Thank you for reading through the first (roughest) draft of this manuscript and for encouraging me to continue writing.

To the saints of The Sanctuary UPC of Fairbanks and the Alaska Yukon District: Thank you for your prayers and for following the prompting of His spirit when I needed a word fitly spoken. Some of you don't even realize you were used of the Lord and how you ministered to me in times of great need. You're such a special group of people and I love you all beyond measure.

Bro. Donnie Copeland and those at Purpose Media Publishing: Thank you for helping me make this dream a reality, and helping extend this book into the hands of someone who may find encouragement in it. Thank you for the late-night reads and brainstorming with little notice. It helped me keep my momentum.

Introduction

Infertility. Or in biblical terms: barrenness. The weight of this word can be crippling. When relying solely on our own strength, many aspects of normal life don't seem to survive the weight of it. As this label is applied to a woman who desires a fruitful womb, self-esteem crumbles, hopes and dreams shatter, marriages and other relationships are often torn to shreds. Words spoken by those seemingly unaware of the often silent and hidden pain of a barren womb plant roots of bitterness in the hearts of the receiver.

A young married female of child-bearing years likely endures frequent questions about when they will begin planning their family. Time passes, and if that woman remains childless, the question becomes more urgent. "Are you guys ever going to have kids?" If you're anything like me and have endured infertility significantly longer than you wanted to (into my late thirties for me), some will conclude that it's just not going to happen. Eventually, they may quit asking, but in some instances, that question is replaced with something like: "With all of the hurting children in this world without a loving mother, I don't know why you can't have a baby." If we're honest, I'd venture to guess we've all asked ourselves and even God that question, perhaps on more than one occasion. As time passes, the weight of barrenness gets heavier and heavier. Leaving your home becomes a minefield. Another weight is added around every corner as if the journey isn't difficult enough to bear.

Imagine waking up another day with the sun shining out your window, a day that is bursting with potential. It is the day the Lord has made, worthy of rejoicing and gladness (Psalm 118:24). You grab your phone and notice there's a notification. Your friend in your hometown texted you with an announcement that she is expecting her second child. She's ecstatic because she just started trying and can't believe how easy it was this time around. And guess what? It's a boy! She just entered the "boy mom" club, one to which you've not been formally invited.

Halfway through your workday, your co-worker asks if you can cover for her while she takes a quick break. She is back from maternity leave and must use the breast pump. After your shift, you go to the grocery store and pass the baby section on your way to get some of the items on your list. All through the store there are small children. As you wait to check out, the lady in front of you is buying diapers for her newborn, and the bagger is gushing over a cute little onesie she bought on sale. When the cashier finally gets to you, she smiles warmly, while inwardly you are praying she doesn't ask you that dreaded question: "Do you have any children?" Noticing your countenance, she awkwardly nods her head, presents you with a sheepish smile, and rings up your groceries in silence. As you try avoiding eye contact, your eyes glance upon the latest version of *Mother & Baby*, with candid photos of newborns sleeping in various arrangements. You can't escape the aching in your heart. There's nowhere to run, or so it seems.

Everywhere you turn, you are reminded of the thing your heart desires most. When you finally get home, a place meant to be a sanctuary from the world, there's an elephant in the room that you and your spouse don't talk about. What is there left to say?

Are you exhausted yet?

This scenario seems hopeless and dark, but it's everyday life for some of us. Does this sound familiar? I sure hope not, but if you're struggling with infertility, you are likely nodding your head in agreement or perhaps even sensing some of the burdensome emotions rising within you that these experiences bring with them.

I have good news for you. *Rest* is available for you. *Hope* can be found in the pages of a book that has far greater worth than the one you're reading. Join me as we walk through the Word and uncover the hidden treasures inside that bring healing to these wounds we've endured along the way. Over the years, I have battled the waves of raw emotions and the weight of this "reality." When I felt like I could bear no more, the pain I experienced led me to the only One who could resolve it, my God. It is my prayer that in sharing my story and my tests of faith, intertwined with the promises in His Word, you will hear Him calling as He draws you closer to Him, and that the Peace that passes all understanding saturates your heart and mind, sustaining you as you endure this season.

It is a great privilege to have you join alongside me as we dive deep into the limitless depths of scripture. Together we will explore the profound beauty of God's design and purpose for women, along with the qualities that He placed within each of us. It is those qualities that portray the essence of His grace, patience, and strength.

"I will say of the LORD, He is my refuge and my fortress: my God; in him will I trust."

Psalm 91:2

1

God Said It Was Very Good

The first commandment God spoke to mankind on the sixth day of creation was to *"be fruitful,* and multiply, and replenish the earth" (Genesis 1:28). Think about this command. Have you ever wondered what significance these words have on our perception of fertility? As I studied this verse, I couldn't help but meditate on these words and contemplate their relevance in my own life. In those early moments of my walk, I wasn't able to fully fathom the profound truths God would reveal to me about myself and the others who walked similar paths long before me. Little did I know these truths would carry me and bring me encouragement to weather one of the darkest seasons of my life.

Allow your mind to paint this picture for a moment. In the heart of the Garden of Eden, our Creator reached His hands into the moist, cool earth which contained every essential element for our bodies, and He meticulously formed us until we bore His image. He deliberately thought of the intricate functions of every cell in our bodies. Our reproductive organs exist for the purpose of multiplying in obedience to this initial command (Genesis 1:28). He is the Giver of Life, yet He awarded us the magnificent honor to reproduce His creation. As He walked with Adam and Eve in the midst of a garden that was bursting with life, God glanced over all that He had made, including Eve's womb, as a father would look upon his newborn for the first time in amazement and awe. When He had taken it all in, there were only two simple words that could be used to describe what was before His eyes: *very good* (Genesis 1:31).

Sickness and infirmities, including infertility, were not a part of God's original plan. All the fruit of the garden apart from one, the fruit of the tree of knowledge of good and evil (Genesis 2:17), would supply the vital nutrients our bodies needed, springing forth from the very earth from which our material bodies were created. The inhabitants of the garden could freely partake of the fruit of the tree of life of which regeneration and longevity were unspoken promises. Barrenness did not exist there. Our genetic make-up was flawless. We were created in the likeness of our God.

Scientists have discovered large animals and plants in the fossil record which allude to a once pristine world thriving with abundant life. The separation of the waters above from the waters below in the beginning of creation created an oxygen-rich environment, and a greenhouse effect which created optimal conditions for all of creation to grow unhindered. No disease or fault could be found in creation – until the day man chose to be disobedient to the one simple request made by our loving God (Genesis 2:17).

Throughout scripture, we see the original design of God's creation was *good*. The Hebrew word for good used in this context is ṭôwb, which signifies everything was in the best state it could be. This word alludes that Creation was beautiful, bountiful, and everything within it was well favored. A modern translation declares that if anything is good, it cannot be weak or defective. It is undamaged and uncorrupted, in a state of perfection and completeness. A woman's womb was created to be *good*.

I know what you're thinking. "How does this perception of goodness reconcile the deep wounds that barrenness has created within us?" God's Word promises us that His thoughts are of peace and not evil when He thinks of us (Jeremiah 29:11). He knows our innermost desires and the hurt we experience waiting for these desires to be fulfilled. He promises to hear us when we call out to Him in times we feel we cannot bear it any longer (Jeremiah 29:12-13). Many times, I have cried out to Him and have clung to promises in scriptures such as Psalm 113:9 which declares "He maketh the barren woman to keep house, and to be a joyful mother of children."

I trusted in His faithfulness, but as years passed, my prayer continued to grow more desperate. I cried out to Him utterly broken, not realizing that He was already moving in ways I couldn't see. His eyes are upon us, and His ears are attune to the very depths of our hearts (Psalm 34:15), knowing exactly what we want to say before we even say it (Matthew 6:8). As I look back through some of the toughest moments, I can see Him there. But why is it seemingly so difficult to see Him when we need to see Him the most, when we are in the thick of the battle and in the midst of what our carnal eyes can only perceive as impossibility?

Not long ago, my husband and I were on a hiking trip with some friends. It was a beautiful day. The trail started at a low elevation by the river. Over the course of a few hours, we gained 3,000 feet. It was a steep uphill trail for about three or four miles. For more than a mile, we walked through thick brush, holding back branches to prevent bushes from smacking us in the face. We couldn't see more than two or three feet in front of us at any given time, but eventually the trail opened up. We walked along a few ridges for a couple of miles. When we reached the highest elevation of our hike, we stopped to see the breathtaking views. I looked out across the ridges and valleys, admiring God's magnificent creation. The way we had traveled suddenly didn't seem as difficult. It was worth it! God spoke to me at that moment and told me that sometimes the toughest trails lead to the most beautiful places. These are the paths not many walk, but those who are brave enough to follow its lead are able to experience the beauty it brings.

In the following chapters of this book, we will walk paths alongside our sisters in the Old Testament, retracing their footsteps through the trials that are unique to them, but very similar to our own. Their testimonies will illuminate the faithfulness of our God and His promise to each of us. It is my prayer that you will see that He who was faithful then is faithful still (Hebrews 13:8). What He did for them, He is able to do for you and me (Romans 2:11).

Just as the natural world has unfulfilled desires – death tirelessly seeks after the living, the desert seeks after rain, and the fire burns relentlessly as long as it's being fed – it is without argument that a barren womb will not be satisfied until it is fruitful (Proverbs 30:16). As we see from the beginning chapters of Genesis, women were created to bring forth life; not just any life, but a living creature who would also bear the image of our God. This astounds me! In fact, Eve, the first woman created, bore the name Chavvàh which literally means "life giver" in

Hebrew. Adam purposefully chose this name "because she was the *mother* of *all living*" (Genesis 3:20). I find it interesting that she was not yet a mother when this word was spoken over her. It was a declaration of faith that what God had spoken surely would come to pass. There was no reason to believe otherwise. God had not been proven unfaithful, and she had no reason not to trust this to be fulfilled.

Unfortunately, there has been a great amount of time and distance from the days of old when man used to walk alongside our God in the garden of His creation. The enemy has learned how to sow seeds of doubt among even the called (Matthew 24:24). Life experiences that seemingly validate this reality make it even more difficult to stand in faith.

"God has, but can He still? And will He – for me?"

I admit there were countless moments along the way when I struggled to understand how my infertility diagnosis fit in the midst of the goodness of God's creation. I was fully convinced that His works truly were marvelous (Psalm 139:13-14) and when I found myself in nature, I couldn't help but feel in awe of all that He had made. During my times of devotion and study, I often wondered if that command was for me, or if it was just for Adam and Eve. But in scripture we find the same command given to Noah's family after the flood (Genesis 9:1). Likewise, it couldn't have been just for them in their day. Man would eventually cease to exist without reproduction.

Some scholars believed it was simply a command to populate the earth, however, this statement disagrees with the rest of the Word of God. Once His words are spoken, God cannot change His mind (see Numbers 23:19, Titus 1:2, and Hebrews 6:18). After those words depart from His mouth, they fulfill what He had spoken (Isaiah 55:11). When God spoke into creation, it simply was. Our bodies were created for conception. God has not changed His mind on that.

I wrestled with scriptures like Psalm 113:9 and others that declared His promises to us, seemingly contradicting what I experienced. At times, I questioned these very scriptures and tried to make the Word of God fit my experience, thinking "surely this is spoken in a general sense and not to me. My situation is different. I'm an exception." I quickly learned that my circumstances, however impossible I perceived them to be, were not strong enough to overcome the power of the Word of God (Hebrews 4:12). Furthermore, God revealed to me that it was man who failed Him; He did not fail man. He had not forsaken me. My barren womb was not a consequence of God withholding His promise or Him failing to keep His Word. It was not a consequence of my sin or my falling short. God is no respecter of persons (Romans 2:11) and we all fall short of the glory of God (Romans 3:23). My barren womb was the result of the fallen state of humanity and its origin was in the Garden of Eden.

In whatever we face in this life, we have a choice to choose a blessing or a curse. Adam and Eve both had a choice. There's a powerful admonition from the Lord in Deuteronomy 30:19, "I call heaven and earth to record this day against you, that I have set before you life and death, blessing and cursing: therefore choose life, that both thou and thy seed may live." God specifically told Adam not to eat of the fruit of the tree of knowledge of good and evil before Eve was formed (see Genesis 2:16-17,21-23).

Second-hand knowledge is not as highly regarded as hearing directly from the source. Has anyone ever spoken a word over you or told you some revelation they had in God's Word? Consider this in a secular sense. If you hear you are about to be blessed with a huge raise from your coworker, you might be skeptical considering how big that blessing is going to be. But if your boss, the one who actually has the power to bring it to pass, says you're getting a raise, well that's a different story. It hits our heart in a different way when we know without a doubt what God had said because *He* is the one who spoke it. There's no evidence in scripture that God warned Eve to beware of this fruit firsthand.

Imagine being in Eve's shoes for the day. You are taking a stroll through the garden exploring all of its awesome wonder. The fragrant aromas of every ripened fruit fill your nostrils and your mouth begins to water. You can taste anything you set your eyes upon, but the tree in the midst of the garden which promises knowledge of all things is forbidden.

Forbidden. What an alluring word.

The struggle between obedience and temptation is palpable. Not to mention there's a snake on the prowl, looking to taint God's flawless creation, His very image. And its weapon was God's Word.

First, the enemy began to question her understanding of the Word of God. Once she entertained his presence, he began to speak contrary to what her husband told her God had said. She allowed this to influence her perspective. The tree was pleasant to look upon and had a wonderfully inviting aroma. According to the voice she allowed to speak into her life, it would give her wisdom and was good for food (Genesis 3:6).

"Why not?" she thought. And before you knew it, she sank her teeth into that juicy fruit.

Adam was no innocent party. He heard the audible voice of God. Yet he allowed his flesh to get in the way and ate of that delicious fruit. Because of their choice, which was in rebellion and defiance to God's authority, death and decay entered God's flawless creation.

True to His Word in Deuteronomy 30:19, all the seed of Adam are affected by his choice; we are the seed of Adam. A barren womb exists because flesh got in the way of promise. Once sin entered the world, the *good* state of our humanity began to deteriorate. God has not forsaken His people. His intentions to us are still good, not evil (Jeremiah 29:11). Humanity has forsaken Him. God is the giver and source of life and conception, and sin resulted in the unfavorable state of a highly favored creation.

When I first discovered this truth, I realized that I couldn't be angry at God for my infertility. If I was, I'd be angry with Him for something He did not do. His plans were for me, not against me. Instead, I could sense His anger at the consequences sin had imposed upon His creation. When I was in prayer, the overwhelming feeling of deep discontentment encompassed my heart as I thought of the fallen state of humanity. There were times His dissatisfaction at the struggles we face in this life was palpable. This changed my perspective on how I viewed myself and my health related to fertility. It also gave me peace of mind knowing that the barren state of my womb was not from living a lifestyle displeasing to the Lord. This perspective propelled me to quench every lie the enemy spoke into my own life (Ephesians 6:16) and the lives of those around me, especially other ladies dealing with infertility.

To reconcile the actions in the garden, God spoke a promise of a Messiah, revealing that He would come to bring salvation of this fallen world and redemption from the curse that started in this chapter of Genesis. God told the enemy He would put enmity, literally hostility and hatred, between him and the woman, as well as between his seed and her seed (Genesis 3:15).

In Genesis 3:16, God told the woman "I will greatly multiply thy sorrow and thy conception; in sorrow thou shalt bring forth children". The first word sorrow is the Hebrew word ʽiṣṣābôn which means labor or pain. The second word sorrow is the Hebrew word ʽēṣeb which means painful toil of body or mind. The grievous pangs just prior to birth fits this description physically. The mental and emotional anguish of an unfulfilled longing for conception is also implied. A barren woman is not exempt from this "curse" simply because her womb is empty. God spoke this to women without respect for persons or circumstances.

Infertility and loss, including miscarriage, still birth, and loss of children after birth can all be tied to these very events in the beginning of creation. God's gift of choice was taken for granted. Man allowed the lusts of the flesh to override the gentle command from God meant to protect us from the devastating effects the wrong choice would call into action. But there's a promise of Redemption! Praise God that He came unto His own and bore our cross so that we could have peace and be free from the weight of sin (2 Corinthians 5:19).

So, what does this have to do with my fertility?

Well, I'm glad you asked!

In our circumstances, we too have a choice. It's true that the situation may look hopeless by the world's standards. For those struggling with infertility, it's likely that report after report shows that our bodies aren't functioning the way they were designed, sometimes without an explanation of why. Thus, we become a statistic, 1 in 6, with specialists who are sometimes unable to offer any options. When they can offer a solution, this path often includes expensive treatments that have little to no guarantee. It can be easy to give in to thoughts of hopelessness, despair, and discouragement. In a worldly sense, we can even justify ourselves in being angry with God. He could intervene. But we must proceed with caution and be diligently aware of the voices that we allow to speak into our lives that in return influence our emotions, thoughts, behaviors, and the choices we make. We must be vigilant, ever guarding our minds, and taking every thought captive that is contrary to God's Word, no matter how validated they may seem by what we see with our natural eyes. Our enemy is a roaring lion seeking whom he may devour, and his intent is to steal, kill, and destroy our God-given purpose (John 10:10, 1 Peter 5:8).

The strategies the enemy used in the garden are not tactics he has forsaken. They are tried and true, and most of the time they work. When Jesus was in the wilderness to be tempted, the enemy referred to Psalm 91:12 when he told Jesus "If thou be the Son of God, cast thyself down: *for it is written,* He shall give his angels charge concerning thee: and in their hands they shall bear thee up, lest at any time thou dash thy foot against a stone" (Matthew 4:6). I can imagine him looking at the Master saying, "Go ahead, throw yourself off the cliff. Let's see if what God said was true." Jesus' response to him was, "It is written again, thou shalt not tempt the Lord thy God" (Matthew 4:7).

"Satan, since you know the word so well, you should also know who you're dealing with. I am the Word. Don't tempt me!"

Just like he did to Eve and to our Lord, the enemy begins by questioning the fulfillment of God's Word in our life experiences and he will use those around us (our healthcare providers, medical science organizations, fertility groups, other ladies with infertility, and even our family and friends) as well as a twisted misrepresentation of scripture to influence our perception of this false portrayal of truth. We must not be distracted by the noise of all that wishes to speak to us in this world. God's Word is ripe and full of promises ready to birth victory in our circumstances. His Word can never be defeated!

There's an overwhelming sense of relief that I have found when I consider God's command to "be fruitful," opposed to the immense responsibility of action that is implied to a woman who is unable to conceive naturally. There's so much pressure to hurry and do whatever it takes at whatever the cost. While the world reminds me time is running out and that I must do something, I have learned to quiet my spirit, allow myself to relax and settle into His presence as I await His prompting and leading. It's in this quietness that He speaks loudest, and we are able to hear Him with the most clarity.

Although it takes a diligent pursuit, we can take those thoughts of hopelessness and worry captive. We can speak light where there is darkness, but we must *choose* to do so. The key lies in knowing Him and His Word and can be summarized into a single word: relationship. When we truly *know* Him, and we've done all we know to do according to His Word, the only thing left to do is stand (Ephesians 6:13). When our strength fails, we can trust and rely on His unfailing strength (2 Corinthians 12:9). When we feel we can no longer carry the burden of the load, He steps in to carry it for us (1 Peter 5:7). When the world doesn't make sense, and we can't find the answers to the questions that plague our mind, we can "be still and know" that He is God, and He is in control (Psalm 46:10). In the end, He will be exalted. "Praise Ye the LORD" (Psalm 113:9).

"And the LORD, he it is that doth go before thee; he will be with thee, he will not fail thee, neither forsake thee: fear not, neither be dismayed."

Deuteronomy 31:8

2

Finding Light in a Dark Place

From the stories of the women in the Bible, to our modern struggles, the thread of God's faithfulness and promises weaves through time, reminding us that He remains the same – our ultimate source of hope and restoration. Though our seasons of life may change, and the challenges they bring come and go, He is constant. We can find comfort in this truth no matter what circumstances we face.

In Isaiah 54, the Lord speaks to Israel, His chosen people, and says "Sing, O barren, thou that didst not bear; break forth into singing" (Isaiah 54:1). To me that seems a little out of place. How can what feels so desolate be so joyful? Or even praiseworthy? The answer is in the promise spoken from God Himself. He promises that the latter end of their journey will be fruitful. Physical famines don't last forever; spiritual famines likewise will end. In Isaiah 54:3, He promises a seed, or offspring from His chosen people, that will include the Gentiles (or simply unbelievers) and that the once desolate places will be thriving with abundant life.

The word barren in this verse is the Hebrew word 'āqār which means one's reproductive organs are sterile or extirpated, simply implying they are unable to bring forth the processes that God originally designed for us to recreate life. Interestingly, the word extirpated literally means this God-given function was rooted out or destroyed completely. This word is the opposite of "to plant." In a physical and spiritual sense, you can't be fruitful if there's no seed planted within you taking root in fertile soil.

Reflecting on the fall of man and the hostility God said He would put between woman and the enemy, as well as the sorrow that would be brought by conception, pregnancy, and labor, this word "barren" seems fitting. From my perspective, barrenness seemed to completely root up and destroy my dreams of becoming a mother, even more so as time passed, and I approached my forties. This was, of course, before God led me on my very recent journey to restored faith, joy, and peace. Yes, one truly can have joy and peace even in a season of barrenness. I will share more about this journey God had led me on in a later chapter.

The first occurrence of this Hebrew word was Genesis 11:30 when scripture tells us of Sarai who was barren and had no children. Similarly, this word was used to describe the barren state of the wombs of Rebekah, Rachel, and Manoah's wife. Each of these ladies had circumstances that labeled their womb as sterile and left their desires for motherhood seemingly rooted up and destroyed. But God sent a word of promise, and reassured these women that He had thoughts of peace, and not of evil (Jeremiah 29:11). This message is echoed throughout the entire Word, so if I seem like a broken record, I'm sorry . . . but I'm not sorry. It's a simple yet profound truth that we often forget to acknowledge. He is for us! We have to believe this and let it sink into the very fibers of our being.

He had prosperous plans for these ladies. He promised their latter end would indeed be greater than their current state. Seasons change. This was a time for weeping and mourning, but soon, there would be a time for laughter and dancing (Ecclesiastes 3:4-5). Our God sees the beginning and the end, and gently guides our steps as we tread through this wilderness season seeing only what is before us. He is our Master Compass.

While writing this book, I came across an author's vlog. E. L. Doctorow wrote:

"Writing is like driving at night in the fog. You can only see as far as your headlights, but you can make the whole trip that way."

Now, if we remove the word "writing" and enter our situation - barrenness (or any trying circumstance that is beyond our understanding) -- the saying is still true. Often, in the trials of this life, it seems as if we can't see more than a few steps ahead. Sometimes it's difficult to even see the *next* step. But we can make this journey to the other side of our circumstances if we follow the Master's lead one step at a time. When we can only see where we are in the moment, we can trust that He sees the end, and He knows the way safely through whatever obstacles come along our way.

We established in the previous chapter that the primary role of women in biblical culture was birthing and raising children. It was actually a shame for a woman to be unable to bear children for her husband. I know I've felt a deep sense of guilt for being unable to conceive and birth the child that would continue my husband's name. His desire from the beginning of our relationship was to be a father. This was a topic of discussion a few days after we decided to start dating. It was a priority. Thankfully, I was equally enthusiastic about having children and we decided to never take any protective measures that would prevent pregnancy from naturally occurring. Neither of us could have ever imagined our first pregnancy would not occur until over fourteen years later, late into our thirties, and end in an early loss.

Unfortunately, maternal and fetal death was very common in biblical times, and some Jewish accounts show that only approximately half of all infants born survived to be five years of age. Thankfully, modern technology and science led us to a place where the mortality rate for mothers and infants have significantly declined since then. However, miscarriage and even still birth rates are still surprisingly high. In fact, one of the things that I heard frequently during my own experience with miscarriage is that "it's very common" for women to miscarry their first pregnancy. I regret how at peace the world is with this fact. Generally, our culture hears of this occurring very frequently, and in return they are quick to accept this as truth and move on. To those who are walking through this, it's not that simple, and in the freshness of the moment when loss occurs, it's not encouraging.

It is tragic.

Devastating.

Seemingly hopeless.

In Exodus 23, God talked to the children of Israel and promised He will send an Angel to keep them in their way and bring them into the promise He prepared for them. This promise was *conditional,* and the children of Israel had a *choice.* God's request from His people was simply this: don't bow down to their gods, don't serve them, and don't live the way they live. He called for separation, a clear distinction between holy and unclean, between light and darkness. If they chose to serve Him, He would bless their food and water, and promised, "I will take sickness away from the midst of thee. There shall nothing cast their young (or miscarry), nor be barren, in thy land" (See Exodus 23:20-26).

This promise is echoed in Deuteronomy 7. "For thou art an holy people unto the LORD thy God: The LORD thy God hath *chosen* thee to be a special people unto himself, above all people that are upon the face of the earth" (Deuteronomy 7:6). They were highly favored! Moses explained to the people that God didn't choose them because they were great in number or for their own power and might; God chose them because He loved them, and He wanted to keep the promise He had spoken to their fathers long ago. "Know therefore that the LORD thy God, he is God, the faithful God, which keepeth covenant and mercy with them that love Him and keep His commandments to a thousand generations" (See Deuteronomy 7:6-10).

I want to encourage you that a thousand generations have yet to be fulfilled! That promise remains for us today. If we keep the conditions of the promise, separation from the idolatry of this world, we have His divine protection. It's a simple loving request with such a great reward.

Some estimate a generation to be about forty years. If that estimation is valid, a thousand generations would be 40,000 years. Even novice students of the Bible can trace the lineage from Adam to Jesus Christ starting in the genealogy accounts from Matthew and Luke, using the names and dates up to the flood found in Genesis, and estimating life spans afterwards until Jesus (Genesis 6:3, Psalm 90:10). This careful study would show that we are approximately 6,000 years from creation in 2023. That's nowhere close to 40,000 years. Folks, the promise still stands! Even if one tried to argue that we are excluded if we are not of Jewish descent, the Word of God declares we were grafted into the children of promise (Romans 11:17)! This promise is for you, and it is for me!

However, as previously mentioned, there are conditions. We must diligently set our heart out to hear the voice of God and be obedient to His will. In response to our obedience, He will keep His covenant and mercy as He promised. "And

He will love thee, and bless thee, and multiply thee: He will also bless the fruit of thy womb . . . Thou shalt be blessed above all people: there shall not be male or female barren among you, or your cattle. And the LORD will take away from thee all sickness, and put none of the evil diseases of Egypt, which thou knowest, upon thee" (See Deuteronomy 7:12-15). Physically and spiritually, Egypt is a place that represents bondage. In our time, Egypt represents the spiritually fallen state of mankind that will continue until Jesus comes for His bride. The culture of the world around us will continue to grow further and further from His original plan (2 Timothy 3:1-13).

Many times throughout scripture God's commandment to His chosen people "come out from among them" or "be ye holy" is echoed. He has continuously aimed to redeem His people, not just for eternal salvation, but from the devastating effects sin has created in our natural lives. He created us for purpose in this life and His will for us is to have joy abundantly.

Our vision can be clouded by the negative reports as well as the questions and worry those reports bring. So if you're hesitant in receiving this for yourself in this moment, it is my prayer that by the time you finish reading this book, you'll be able to experience the peace that can come in the waiting, and use this time wisely by drawing closer to Him with a deeper level of intimacy, knowing that God is not a man that He should lie, and is a faithful to His Word, especially to those who diligently seek him (Hebrews 11:6). God alone holds the power to open or close the womb. He knows where you are, and you are in good hands.

> "The LORD is my strength and my shield; my heart trusted in him, and I am helped: therefore my heart greatly rejoiceth; and with my song will I praise him."
>
> Psalm 28:7

3

An Echoed Promise

Labels: the world is full of them, and we apply them to everything. It's often how we remember certain people, places, events, things, etc. We group ideas together and slap on a sticker that summarizes them in often a single word. Think about this: how would you feel if the very first thing someone knew about you was that you had a barren womb?

As I previously mentioned, the first time this word "barren" is noted in scripture, is to describe one woman. Second only to being Abraham's wife, it's the first thing we learn about her. But she has such a powerful story to tell! It's a testimony of God's faithfulness. However, all we know for a while about this amazing woman is that she is unable to bear children. Genesis 11:29-30 simply states "the name of Abraham's wife was Sarai . . . But Sarai was barren; she had no child."

Since she is the first woman recorded in scripture bearing the label of infertile, she likely had no predecessors, no other women of promise she could read about in the Word of God who through the power of God Almighty overcame their circumstances. There were no previous accounts recorded that she could cling to for hope and encouragement. She didn't even have the promise in Exodus and Deuteronomy we spoke about in the previous chapter. In fact, these books were not even written. People in her day relied directly on the spoken word. Imagine how hopeless her journey may have seemed to her.

I find it fascinating to look at biblical timelines that estimate the year of birth and death of these amazing men and women of Old Testament times. It gives us a great picture of just how God's word spread throughout His people. Although it was a vast amount of time, longer lifespans meant that historical accounts such as Creation and the flood were not diluted over and over by games of "telephone." Likely little was lost in the accuracy of what was spoken. For perspective of how much time had passed, think about this: Abraham was the 19th generation from Adam, and many of the men between these two men, or at least their sons and daughters were still walking the earth. If the story got twisted somehow, someone would have corrected them.

Perhaps there were some stories of women miraculously healed by God's mighty hand, but there are no scriptural accounts that record it. She didn't have any hope of a resolution to hold on to when the road became long and lonely.

She was almost 100 years old, by the way.

And we think our journey is long!

I've told the Lord more than once, "Please don't make me a Sarai! I mean, I do want the will of God for my life, but, if possible, Lord (and all things are possible with You!), can it come a little earlier? Pretty please?"

"Like . . . *now*, Lord?"

Really though! Isn't it this way with anything we are waiting on God for?

God promised Sarai's husband that he would be blessed with a huge family, so much so that they would become a great nation, and through him all the families of the world would also be blessed (Genesis 12:2 - 3). She was approximately 65 years old when that promise was spoken (Genesis 12:4, 17:17). Although men and women in her time lived significantly longer than the average lifespan now and it was likely normal to conceive much later in life because of this, at some point during her waiting the reproductive process within her body ceased (Genesis 18:11). How could it be possible that she would be the vessel God would use to keep His promise to her husband? There must be some other way, right? The promise was to Abraham. Perhaps she misunderstood?

There's no account of Sarai being aware of the details of that promise until *just before* she conceived Isaac many years later when she heard the promise firsthand from the voice of God Himself. How many times does that happen in our lives? We are waiting for God to move in what seems like eternity with time standing still while it moves on for everyone around us, but then – all of a sudden there it is, the promise is being fulfilled right before our eyes.

Similar to Eve, God had spoken to her husband face to face and gave him instructions: if Abraham would come out from among his family, out of his country, and follow God's lead, he would be fruitful and father many nations of people that would span across the entire world. It's without a doubt Sarai's desire for motherhood burned within her heart just like it burns within ours. She likely lost sleep and felt the pangs of emptiness and the void within her that no one around her could quite understand. She knew our struggle. She was a woman, and this desire is natural *and obedient* to that first command God had spoken to mankind. However, she had to rely and trust on the words of her husband as she didn't hear from God herself. Oh, how difficult is that to do sometimes! Has someone ever spoken a word from God over you? You have faith and want to receive it, yet somehow, it's so difficult to believe!

Jesus was with His disciples sometime after the mount of transfiguration when a man came to Him saying he had a son who was tormented by an evil spirit. His apostles couldn't cast the spirit out of the child and the father was desperate. Falling at the feet of Jesus, the man cried out, "if You can do anything, have compassion on us and help." Jesus responded, "If you can believe, all things are possible to him that believes." The man's response? "Lord, I believe, but help my unbelief" (See Mark 9). In other words: "Lord, I believe you can! It's within Your power and ability. Help me to believe You can – *for me*!"

I'm so thankful for a God who speaks to us, but there are situations where it seems like He is silent. In those moments we need to trust in the written and spoken Word, and the men and women of God He has placed in our lives. Admittedly, that is not always an easy task, especially when it seems your prayers are being unanswered.

Obedient to God's word, Sarai's family moved from Haran and stopped in the land of Canaan, the promised land. Again, God met with Abraham and echoed His promise to make him a father of many nations. In response to what God had spoken, Abraham built an altar there unto the Lord in the land of the promise before the promise was even fulfilled.

An altar is a place of sacrifice – or surrender. It is symbolic of taking off our perceptions and expectations and in exchange saying "Lord, Your will be done." Sarai likely walked past that altar. Her eyes possibly had rested upon it as she considered the details of the promise that were yet to be surrendered. Each day that passed there was a memorial that reminded her of what God had spoken over her family. Sarai likely allowed her mind to run with wild abandon, daydreaming of how this promise would manifest in their lives and in what timing this would be brought to pass.

I have planned many of the moments in my mind surrounding when I'd conceive: how I would notify my husband, our parents, our family, our church, and our friends. I've daydreamed of holding my newborn and tried to muster up some sense of what that might feel like. She was no different than I am. She was created to be a mother and her womb was empty.

Sarai was beautiful and well favored, even at an age older than 65 (Genesis 12:11, 14). Her family had gathered quite a bit of sustenance along their way. As they journeyed south from city to city, surely she wondered if the next stop would be her chance to conceive. All along the journey God continued to confirm His promise to her husband. She probably continued to hear from her husband how the Lord had spoken, but still had no details of how this would affect her. She was time and time again left to her own imagination. What a dangerous place that can be! It's funny how we allow our minds to wander and write the narrative when all God really wants is for us to just be still and trust that He is God, and that He has this all under control (Psalm 46:10). I can't blame her. This is our humanity at work. Sometimes our imaginations are our worst enemy and after many different rewrites of the same story in my own mind, I've found myself wondering why I don't just leave it in His hands. In the end, I can see that His way is always better than mine.

Sometimes in our journey we can get a little off course. A famine in Canaan caused Sarai and her family to seek the comforts of Egypt. The lack of food supply in the land would prove to be very uncomfortable and difficult, but there's no evidence that Egypt was ever a part of God's plan. It's interesting that God calls him to a place that seems to be "a dry and thirsty land where no water is" (Psalm 63:1) and instead of trusting that God has a plan for redemption of these current circumstances, Abraham leads his family away from the land of promise to chase the land with "greener grass," so to speak. Isn't that a common reaction when things don't go according to our plan? God has a way of getting us a little uncomfortable so that we learn to rely on Him for strength, but that pressure often causes us to seek ways to help ourselves.

I often struggled with waiting. I was aging and my biological clock was ticking. I considered all of the world's possibilities. We had many ultrasounds, procedures, fertility medications to stimulate ovulation, what felt like thousands of blood tests, and had consults with several different providers. I even researched adoption over and over again, despite my husband's adamancy that this was not something he felt would be best for our family. Once God opened my womb and I experienced pregnancy for the first time, which as I mentioned previously had ended in an early loss, the physician assistant (PA) we saw offered a word of hope: "You're more fertile following a miscarriage."

Once again, we were presented with more options: Clomid or Letrozole to stimulate eggs to mature and grow in the ovaries and then artificial insemination right into the uterus to ensure the "best chance possible" at conception! Why wait? As soon as the next cycle starts, we can get started right away! Well, this does sound hopeful. Right? But there was that aching in my heart once again. There was another option she had not considered.

Not long after my miscarriage, our PA, who was incredible, referred us to maternal-fetal medicine in Anchorage, Alaska to be seen prior to conception as I had some rare health concerns and she wanted to be proactive. The provider I saw told me I would be at an increased risk of postpartum hemorrhage due to my condition. If I took Clomid or Letrozole, which he told me would be relatively safe for me to do so, I would have a slightly increased chance of multiples (twins, triplets, or beyond) which would increase the risk of bleeding even further.

So here I was with a decision: I could take the Letrozole, which had less of a chance of multiples than Clomid, pray that I don't have multiples or that I don't have a life-threatening postpartum hemorrhage if I do – or I could just choose to not take anything and pray for God to open my womb *again*.

Either choice required faith in God to intervene and protect me. It's the same measure of faith! Do I do all that I can to achieve this in *my* timing? Or do I wait and truly trust that God sees me and has a plan for even this?

Sarai, too, had to make a difficult decision. First, let me journey a little off course to give you some background information. Once her family arrived in Egypt, Abraham feared the Egyptians would kill him because Sarai was so lovely to look upon. He devised a plan to lie and told Sarai to say she was his sister. His fear was unnecessary, though. His God had given him a promise that had not yet come to pass, and He had not failed him yet. Fear cancels out our faith; the two cannot coexist. If we truly believe God is our provider, then we must act upon that faith when we need Him to be that the most, not just when we are overflowing with sustenance from natural means.

As Abraham suspected, Pharaoh looked upon Sarai's fair countenance, blessed him abundantly with livestock and servants as a form of payment or dowry, and then took her into his home. As a penalty, God sent plagues upon Pharaoh and all that were with him. Realizing his fault, Pharaoh commanded them to leave and sent them away with all that they had, including all he had given them for Sarai. This family came into the land a blessed nation, and they left with abundantly more. God is able to work all things out for our good (Romans 8:28). Sadly, exposure to Egypt and its culture had tacked on some heavy unintended baggage.

This is an interesting twist in Sarai's story, because someone entered their lives in Egypt. Scripture doesn't exactly state when Hagar started tagging along for the journey, but the Bible does mention she was their handmaiden and that she was an Egyptian (Genesis 16:1).

After departing from Egypt, it's interesting that Abraham went back to Bethel, the place where he had first built that altar to the Lord (Genesis 13:3). God has a way of waiting patiently for us to return to where we went astray. Once back in Bethel, Lot and Abraham finally parted ways. God had told him in the beginning of his journey to depart from all of his father's kindred, but he didn't object when his nephew Lot tagged along. Therefore, Abraham hadn't been completely obedient to what the Lord asked of him. While from our perspective it seemed to have delayed his promise, God did not withhold it. This detour did not catch God off guard! I am so thankful for His grace as well as His patience to allow us to grow those spiritual muscles we need to live life as abundantly as He planned. Just as an infant has to fall down and try again multiple times before it eventually learns to stand, and then to walk, we also have to learn to walk by faith and not by sight (2 Corinthians 5:7).

With the slate clear, a fresh altar with a rekindled fire, and a clear conscience with God, the Lord reappeared to Abraham and reconfirmed His promise. He showed him the land that all of the nations that would come out of his future children would possess.

The promise still stands, Abraham.

God did not go back on His word!

It seems Abraham was patiently waiting all these years and was satisfied with gentle reminders from the Lord that He would fulfill His promise. However, Sarai still had not heard from the Lord herself. Her body continued to grow older, and all natural signs of her fertility came to cease. As the journey continued to grow longer and longer, at some point she allowed her heart to come to terms with not bearing children of her own. Perhaps there was even a point where she grew to accept this in order to protect herself from the emptiness she felt.

I wish I could say I don't know what this is like. There have been times when I asked myself "do I even still want this?" It seemed the older I grew and the further I seemed to be from my youthful twenties, I began to question if it even still mattered to me. I would often criticize myself for even thinking about wanting to conceive. Sometimes we are our worst enemies! One thing I have learned in this journey is how to force myself to be "okay" as a defense mechanism. In fact, recently as I was navigating the extreme grief of my loss on top of the grieving process for several other areas of my life that were seemingly out of control, I realized that when someone asks me "Are you okay?" or "How are you?" I would often answer with "Yes" or "I'm okay."

And the sad thing is – I meant it.

I learned to be okay not being okay, and I was comfortable that way. It became the new normal, the new me, so to speak.

After time passed, the Lord visited Abraham "in a vision, saying, Fear not: I am thy shield, and thy exceeding great reward." In a boldness that could only come from a rekindled relationship with God, he asked, "Lord God, what wilt thou give me, seeing I go childless" (Genesis 15:1-2). This seems to be the point where he was growing a little tired of waiting himself. "God, you promised me, and I haven't seen it come to pass yet." The promise keeps coming, and there's a great expectation that it's right around the corner, yet time passes and there's no fulfillment. I know that feeling all too well and I can't fault him for boldly declaring "Now's as good of a time as any, God. You promised! What are you going to do about this?" But there was an altar in his life, and he had a personal connection with God. In fact, their bond was so intimate that God said "I know him. He'll teach his children my ways" (Genesis 18:19). God trusted him.

Prayer and divine intervention are the answers to barrenness, spiritually and physically, and he knew God was the supplier of all of his needs. Abraham knew Him well enough that he could be bold enough to approach Him in this way. Just as a loving father reassures his discouraged child, God prompts him to look out upon the vast night sky at the innumerable amount of stars and says "so shall your seed be" (Genesis 15:5).

"And he believed in the Lord" (Genesis 15:6).

"And so, after he had patiently endured, he obtained the promise."

Hebrews 6:15

4

It May Be

After they had been in the land of Canaan (the promised land) ten years, Sarai considered the words she had heard God had spoken. She had given up hope that she would ever have her chance to conceive and carry her own child in her own womb, but God had promised her husband children! One day, Sarai was thinking about that promise, and remembered the Egyptian slave girl they had picked up along their journey as well as some customs she'd observed. She tells her husband "It *may be* that I may obtain children *by her*" (Genesis 16:2). Was she being impatient and trying to take the matter into her own hands like some think, or was she simply trying to find the will of God?

"It may be."

How many times do we ask this same question trying to fill in the narrative of our own promise?

This phrase doesn't seem to fit the picture of someone who is trying to have their own way over the way of God. He hasn't spoken directly to her yet and she is having to go off the little pieces of information that Abraham is telling her, "There's a promise." How many times do we try to fill in the rest of the missing pieces? And when we do, how often does it turn out exactly like we think it will? Our minds are finite, but God's is infinite. There are no limitations to His capabilities, but when the waiting is long, our mind tries to play with all sorts of scenarios, and we begin testing all the doors to see which one is open.

"It may be" this one.

I can't fault Sarai for this! She's a woman with a God-given purpose whose very nature was to be a mother, and God had spoken a promise of children to her husband. She didn't understand, and she didn't have the Word of God telling her not to lean on her own understanding.

"I wonder if this is how it's supposed to happen?" she thought.

I've definitely had my "it-may-be" moments. My husband and I moved to Fairbanks in December 2016. Before the move, I worked for a residential treatment facility for children diagnosed with autism, down syndrome, obsessive compulsive disorder (OCD), and attention deficit hyperactivity disorder (ADHD), to name a few. Often these children were victims of abuse. I connected with a child in the facility whose guardian was the state, and on some holidays like Thanksgiving I would bring him home with me to celebrate with my family. When I moved to Alaska. I was able to keep in contact and occasionally pick him up when visiting back home.

In 2018, after over ten years of struggling to become pregnant and a few failed attempts with infertility medications, I went home for a week and was able to visit with this child. Coincidentally, the child's caseworker who was his legally appointed guardian was visiting. Staff at this center would frequently make comments like "you should adopt him." I would always reply with, "I would in a heartbeat," but I knew that it would be a challenge. On this particular occasion, those comments were made, and the guardian wanted to speak to me in this very regard. She knew that I was going to be in town and that I would be picking him up on this day.

I had never met this woman in person. We were familiar with each other, but only through emails while I cared for him as a patient previously as well as this recent contact. My visits with him had to have her approval. She pulled me into a room with another woman present and asked me about my interest in adopting him. I want to point out that prior to our move in 2016, my husband and I were not living for God. However, shortly after coming to Alaska, I completely surrendered to the truth, and my husband followed not long after. On this particular occasion, we were both living for God with all that we had and were both in ministry.

I told the woman that I would adopt him in a heartbeat, but there were some challenges. My husband had a non-violent record from when he was eighteen which resulted in a felony charge. I also lived across the country, more than 4,200 miles, and wouldn't be able to foster him until adoption occurred. If I remember correctly, the preference of the team I worked for was to foster first, allowing them to ensure it was a good fit for permanent placement. We had no intention of moving back to my home state at any time in the near future. What I didn't mention was that my husband was not thrilled with the idea of adoption, and I have to admit I was a little worried as well as the child hadn't really connected with my husband other than saying a few words at family dinners where they both were present.

She assured me that the adoption process could be expedited, and she would look into allowing me to foster him out of state. This was almost unheard of! She also told me that my husband's background would not be an issue and they would help us work out the difficulties with the distance. My heart soared and sank at the same time. On one hand, this was my opportunity. I had often daydreamed of what it might be like to take in this broken child and love him abundantly.

"It may be."

It really appeared to me that God was working out all the details on my behalf. The process seemed like it would go seamlessly. On the other hand, my husband was not going to be on board, and I knew that. I dreaded even having this conversation with him.

"How could I get him on board?" I thought.

Then the rational God-fearing voice within me spoke.

"If it truly was the plan of God, I wouldn't have to. God would work it out."

I worked in the emergency department at the time and upon my return from that trip, I spoke with a social worker with whom I frequently worked. I knew that behavioral health resources in Fairbanks were extremely limited, especially for children and adolescents, and the situation was no better anywhere else in the state. In case you didn't know, Alaska is huge! Everyone who thinks everything is bigger in Texas hasn't been to Alaska. Actually, the entire state of Texas can fit inside of Alaska and there's still plenty of room to add a few more states in there.

I digress.

Needless to say, I worried that if there were ever any problems with his behavior that I wouldn't be able to give him the support he needed. In my heart, I knew this was not going to work. But the timing of all of this was so "coincidental" that I thought for sure it was the will of God. Sadly, it's not the first time I thought this and was wrong.

My husband and I went for breakfast one morning and I began to tell him what happened. He was adamant that we would not do this. I became angry with him! I prayed, "God, I know you can change his heart." What I didn't realize was God was using this as an opportunity to change mine.

One day while I was home and Joey was at work, I came to terms with the fact that I had to submit to my husband's will and notify the state guardian that WE had decided this was not in our (anyone involved) best interests and *we* decided *we* should not go through with the adoption.

I couldn't say the words out loud because I disagreed, and it was emotionally devastating to even think of including myself in the "we" of that decision.

. . . but submission isn't *submission* if you agree.

Ouch!

That was a painful lesson. I spent what felt like an entire day in my spare bedroom turned prayer room, and I pleaded with the Lord. I remember screaming and writhing in a fetal position in agony with groanings that could not be uttered (Romans 8:26). I was in physical, emotional, and spiritual agony. I'm so thankful for the Holy Ghost in moments like these, when we don't have the words to say the Spirit makes intercession for us. This is where the true trial of my faith in God's promise began. Little did I know, He was leading me on my own wilderness journey, and although this *was* a very dark time, it became one of the most beautiful experiences of my life and showed me the true nature and glory of just how wonderful and *awe*-some our God really is!

Because I could not bear to utter those words over the phone, I typed out an email, called Joey, and read it to him for his approval.

"One more time, God." I thought. "One more chance to change his heart before I press send."

When I got him on the phone, he told me it didn't matter what the email said, but I explained to him my weakness at this moment, and that I needed him to verbally tell me to hit the send button. It seemed as if all time stood still for the short moment before he uttered the words.

"Send it."

Realizing God was calling me into a place of obedience and submission, my finger pressed the button. My heart broke into what felt like a million irreparable pieces.

Thankfully, I know the Potter.

I remember wrestling within myself after that moment. It was like David while he waited for his child to die. He fasted and sat in mourning until the word came that the child was dead. Then he got up, dusted himself off, and went on with his life. Except, I didn't know what to do next. Remember the analogy of driving through the fog? Sometimes we don't even know what the next step is in our journey. Again, God is our Master Compass leading us according to His perfect will. I felt led to read the Word of God, but honestly had no desire. I felt Him drawing me, but I didn't want to talk to God or even hear what He had to say. I wanted to go to sleep and withdraw from the day.

Here's my journal entry from that moment with emphasis added for context:

January 15, 2019:

I let [the child] go. After fighting with myself and God, wondering where my answer was and why I felt the way I did, why He hasn't spoken to me [at least in the way I had wanted Him to], I was led to read Judges 13. . .

In a later chapter I will discuss more about why Judges 13 is so significant to my story and how God continues to use it to remind me of His promise.

Is this a coincidence that I read that after I asked God where He was and why He hasn't spoken to me? I fought [within] myself as to [whether or not I should] read a book, sleep, read the word, etc. And when I finally gave in, there it was.

The voice of God with a message just for me.

If this was JUST A COINCIDENCE, then all the other encounters I thought I had with God are a coincidence. If that's true, then God hasn't spoken to me. If God hasn't spoken to me, then . . . what?

I'm hanging on to this promise, God.

That last statement brings tears to my eyes as I reflect on the intense rawness of those painful moments.

Such powerful faith!

I knew my relationship with God was so real and that He *does* speak with me. I know His voice. I could have chosen at that moment to allow my frustrations to drive a wedge between us, but I chose instead to believe that His plan for me is greater than my plan for me. Looking back, I can see that adopting this child was not in God's plan. There is a crisis for behavioral health services for children in Alaska, and that child did go on to be adopted, which I've heard had a lot of challenges. It would not have been in his best interest to take him from a place that he was thriving to a new place, with new people far from what he knew, and have no support. On another level, I think about what it could have done to my marriage.

I'm thankful God brought me to a place where, although painful, I could *let go and let Him have His way.*

Sarai needed to get to this place, too, but in her sincere desire to find the will of God, she was stuck on her interpretation of His will – "It may be." So, she gave her servant girl to her husband to have children for her. Although this may make absolutely no sense to us now as to how this could be a viable solution, this was not an abnormal custom for a barren woman to do in her day. I have to give her credit, she waited eleven years, ten of those years being in the land where the promise was supposed to be fulfilled. Day after day, in the very place where God had declared her husband would have children as innumerable as the stars, she desperately waited for it to come to pass.

Abraham must have been considering the details of how this would be fulfilled as well, because when Sarai said, "the LORD hath restrained me from bearing: I pray thee, go in unto my maid; *it may be* that I may obtain children by her," he considered his wife's suggestion and chose to act upon it (Genesis 16:2). It seemed like a good solution to him, too. He didn't reject her request and reassure her of God's promise. He willingly complied. God didn't spell out the details to him either, right? He simply said, "you'll have many offspring, Abraham."

Yikes!

What a mess we can make of things when relying on our own understanding.

Hagar conceived and immediately there was tension between these two women. The plan did not quite go the way Sarai had expected. What should have brought peace and joy brought strife and contention, and with it regret and remorse. She thought it would fill that aching void within her heart, yet there it was still, and now she had to deal with all of this.

It's funny – yet tragic – how we write the narrative sometimes.

God simply says He will, and instead of settling in our heart that He is a man of His Word, we ask a bunch of questions. We want the how, why, when, where, what, and with who. But God just wants us to wait and see, being content in what He has spoken, knowing it shall come to pass.

It's the holiday season as I write this, and I imagine being a young child with a gift in a box covered with fancy wrapping paper. We shake it, feel its weight, and wonder what is inside, anticipating the day that we get to open it up and see! We know the day will come. There should be no question about that. There's no worry or anxiety; just joy and expectation. If only we could wait in such a way as adults, right?

After an additional thirteen years of waiting, and living with the circumstances of their choice, God made a covenant with Abraham, promising another time to make him the father of many nations, and to be His God, and the God of his seed. "God said unto Abraham, as for Sarai thy wife, thou shalt not call her name Sarai, but Sarah shall her name be. And I will bless her, and she shall be a mother of nations; kings of people shall be of her." (Genesis 17:15-16). Abraham had completely given up on the chance of Sarah ever conceiving. Her reproductive years appeared to be over in a natural sense, and Abraham now had Ishmael. For all he knew his promise was already on its way to fulfillment. Was he not the promised son? Did the Lord not realize that Sarah was 90 years old? "This is impossible, God. Let Ishmael live out this promise and give him your favor" (Genesis 17:18).

But God repeated His promise again: "Sarah thy wife shall bear thee a son indeed; and thou shalt call his name Isaac: and I will establish my covenant *with him* for an everlasting covenant, and with his seed after him."

I find it interesting that all throughout the lineage of Jesus there are barren women. To me, it seems like God is using this as a testimony that He is the ultimate judge, and He has the final say! He uses sinners, harlots, gentiles, and barren women as His chosen vessels to carry forward the seed of promise: His chosen people which would ultimately bring forth the birth of the Messiah. It doesn't matter who or what you think you are, or even what this world says you are. The labels (or diagnosis) applied to your name, even on a medical chart somewhere, do not limit God. He can use you and He can use your circumstances. It's such a beautiful sentiment of the heart of our great and awesome God! We are highly favored!

A short time later, the Lord visited Abraham again with two angels looking for Sarah who was in the tent. He told him, "I will certainly return to thee according to the time of life; and lo, Sarah thy wife shall have a son." Sarah overheard the conversation from her tent and immediately disbelief began to speak to her. Scripture states she actually "laughed within herself" (Genesis 18:12). The Lord knew her thoughts, and He responded, "Is anything too hard for the Lord?" He then confirmed His promise and declared "at the time appointed," – in other words in His perfect timing, the time He has in mind for His plan to be fulfilled the way He wants it to be – Sarah will conceive (see Genesis 18:9-14). And she did. God had delivered on His promise "as He had spoken" (Genesis 21:1).

The promise was born more than 25 years after it had been spoken, in a time that it seemed it was impossible.

By natural standards it was.

But our God is not bound by the natural.

If He has given you a promise, it shall come to pass; it's His nature, and it's His Word. He is the Promise Keeper and always keeps the covenants he makes with His people. Waiting is difficult, especially when we don't know the whats, whens, and hows. But one day He will deliver on that promise "as He had spoken."

"For all the promises of God in him are yea, and in him Amen, unto the glory of God by us."

2 Corinthians 1:20

5

Passionate Desire

One night, I was reading an unrelated book as I was contemplating how I wanted to lay out the stories of Rebekah and Rachel, and I came across the word "desire." I love the old 1828 version of Webster's dictionary. Many of the definitions listed in that version contain scriptural references to validate their interpretation of any word to be correct. This timeless resource describes the word desire as:

"An emotion or excitement of the mind directed to the attainment or possession of an object from which pleasure (sensual, intellectual, or spiritual) is expected; a passion excited by the love of an object, or *an uneasiness at the want of it*, and directed to its attainment or possession. *Desire is that internal act, which, by influencing the will, makes us proceed to action.*"

That seems pretty powerful.

I'd say this description accurately describes what a woman trying to conceive her first child feels, especially after a season of barrenness. It depicts a strong emotional state of mind with an uneasy expectation that influences our will and drives us to do literally anything to fulfill it. As the journey continues, desperation may cause us to re-evaluate some of our boundaries and the lengths we will go to get our heart's desire. Think about nature. When a mother bear and her cub are foraging for food and some predator comes along potentially threatening her baby, the mother bear will aggressively contend for her cub. As women, destined to be mothers by God's design, we too can be aggressive in our attempts to defend our children or fight for a chance to conceive a child. I have seen so many women risk their finances and even their relationships with their spouse in a desperate attempt to do whatever it takes at whatever the cost. I wish I could say I don't know what it's like to be in their shoes, that I've never considered risking anything and everything just for *a chance.*

For a little bit of biblical context, Sarah had died and Isaac, the promised son, was mourning over the loss of his mother, so Abraham sent his servant to his homeland and his father's family to pick a suitable wife in an attempt to comfort him. When the servant came to the city of Abraham's brother Nahor, he rested at a well and called upon his master's God (Genesis 24:12-14). Before he finished praying, Rebekah came to draw water. His prayer had been answered exactly the way he requested.

Rebekah was God's chosen helpmeet for the child of promise, and she wouldn't have made it on the pages of this book you're holding if her story didn't mimic ours in some way. She was a woman of a fair countenance and had great character. Without hesitation, she allowed the servant to drink and offered to give the animals water as well. She had a servant's heart.

Once Abraham's servant realized God answered his prayer immediately and exactly as he asked, he fell down and worshiped Him, proclaiming "Blessed be the LORD God of my master Abraham, who hath not left destitute my master of his mercy and his truth" (Genesis 24:27).

I'm not certain what sparked her attention: the mentioning of Abraham's name or the mention of the Lord miraculously guiding this servant to her family. I believe it was likely both. Whatever the cause, upon witnessing the way the servant responded, Rebekah immediately ran to tell her family of the events that just unfolded before her eyes. She told of how God miraculously provided for this servant at their well and how she was the chosen vessel that God would use to carry out His will. Her brother, Laban, ran back to the well and addressed the servant as "thou blessed of the Lord" (verse 31).

Abraham's kindred were apparently no stranger to the God of Abraham. Perhaps they had heard their elders mention Abraham who departed the land years ago, and perhaps they knew he became prosperous at the hand of the Lord. Or perhaps they, too, had a personal relationship with Him. Whatever the cause, they knew that the current arrangement was made by God Himself, and they had hearts that sought to be obedient to Him.

Rebekah may have been a chosen vessel indeed, but she also had to make a choice. She had to be willing to leave everything she knew to marry a man she had never met in a land she'd never been. That seems like quite a sacrifice, not to mention risky! Without question, Rebekah simply states "I will go" (Genesis 24:58). My interpretation of that is: "Yes, Lord. I will do whatever You ask of me. Use me for Your honor and Your glory." She was willing no matter the outcome or the details and was all in.

No questions asked.

No requests or conditions.

Just submission.

This willingness to surrender her expectations and wants allowed God to do His perfect work unhindered.

After making her way through all of the "goodbyes" to the members of her family, they proclaimed a blessing over her saying, "be thou the mother of thousands of millions" (verse 59). They had no clue what the Lord had in store for her. And it came to pass that she *was* the mother of millions of descendants. Her son would be the father of an entire nation, Israel, and generations of her seed likely continue on to this day. Furthermore, out of her lineage came the promised Messiah, Almighty God in the flesh (Luke 3:34).

As the years passed by, it became evident that she was barren. I'm so thankful that's not how her story ended. Knowing Who his help was, her husband Isaac went to intercede on her behalf and the Lord answered that prayer. He was Abraham's promised son by which the entire world would be inhabited. Isaac knew the power of his God. He was there when God asked his father to sacrifice his promised son on the altar, and when his father's obedience aligned with the will of God, Isaac was there.

He was the one who laid bound upon the altar (Genesis 22:1-18).

And he witnessed God deliver him mightily. Before that event had taken place, Isaac saw his father's faith as they walked up that same mountain together. He witnessed his father's steadiness, a calm assurance that God would provide Himself a sacrifice on that altar that day, and that the two of them would return from that mountain together to worship Him when it was all through.

In the end, God would be exalted.

Isaac knew without a doubt that His God was a *faithful* God.

There were some memorials built in his mind and some stones piled up in a place he called Beth-el, where God spoke a word of promise to him. He could visit those places mentally and physically to gain strength. When he was discouraged, he could look upon these memorials he built and remember the faithfulness of the God he served.

Do you have any memorials in your life where God had clearly spoken something over you or to you? Something that perhaps has yet to come to pass?

Faith is the material portion of everything we hope for, and the evidence of things we don't see in our natural eyes (Hebrews 11:1). Faith does not come when something is present in our lives nor are we exercising faith when we can use our senses to validate that what we desire exists, but it is the substance that is present *in lieu of* this. Faith is that peace we feel that states, "God, you spoke it and I believe it will come to pass."

It's the placeholder.

Once again, God was true to His Word. Rebekah indeed conceived and another barren womb was miraculously opened by the hand of the God of all power. What a faithful God He is indeed! At some point, however, Rebekah felt something not quite right within her womb. What a dreadful feeling this is. You finally experience the joy of receiving what your heart desires most, yet somehow it feels so uncertain. God heard her petition. He came through. She could feel the proof moving inside of her. She knew she had a blessing spoken over her life to be the mother of thousands of millions. Likewise, her husband's seed was promised to be as the stars of the sky (Genesis 26:4). Unlike Sarah and Abraham, this time the promise was spoken over both parties in the marriage covenant individually. It seemed less room for error of interpretation. So why are there all of these struggles in her womb, threatening the very life of her promise and potentially her own? It's obvious the commotion was worrisome to her. "If I'm supposed to be the mother of millions, why is this pregnancy in such turmoil?" Anyone who has had an impending loss of pregnancy can relate. I certainly can.

Quickly after I found out God had answered my prayer of more than fourteen years, I was deeply grieved by the possibility of losing it. I had a week of pure bliss, an extreme thankfulness of God's miraculous intervention, without a doubt in my mind that God would bring it to fulfillment. In fact, I truly felt my pregnancy was invincible and we began telling everyone that would listen on the day we found out. I was approximately five weeks pregnant at that time. It was a miracle by His very hand. And I *know* my God! I felt highly favored by this blessing God gave me for a season. Then about a week later, things slowly began to go wrong, and my pedestal was pulled right out from under me. I hit rock bottom like a ton of bricks.

There's a song by Sis. Shara McKee called "The Anchor Holds" that describes best what I felt in those moments awaiting the impending loss of our first pregnancy:

"I've had visions

And I've had dreams

I've even held them in my hand

But I never knew

They would slip right through

Like they were only grains of sand

The Anchor holds

Though the ship is battered

The Anchor holds

> Though the sails are torn
>
> And I have fallen on my knees
>
> As I faced the raging seas
>
> The Anchor holds
>
> In spite of the storm
>
> ...
>
> But it was in the night
>
> Through the storms of my life
>
> Oh that's where God proved His love to me"

If it wasn't for those memorials I built in my mind and heart before this moment, I don't think I could have made it through. My pastor, Reverend G. A. Parrish, often admonished us from behind the pulpit to set up memorials from the high points in life so that when the fierce winds of life blow, we would be anchored in what we knew to be tried and true, the faithfulness of God. It's a true depiction of being anchored in a faith in Him who is steadfast and unwavering; He who is constant, never-changing, and never fails.

And that anchor holds!

It doesn't matter what this journey or any other trial in this life brings our way, as long as we know from where our help comes. He saw me through. Likewise, Rebekah ran to the Lord for answers. He assured her that she would give birth to twins. He explained to her that she had two babies that would be two different nations in her womb, and there would long be conflict between those nations. This was the struggle she felt already. She needed not to worry. He had it all under control. Her pregnancy would be successful. And it was!

Similar to Sarah, Rebekah had to wait almost 20 years for her promise to be fulfilled (Genesis 25:20, 26). This makes me feel like my years of waiting aren't completely abnormal, despite what traditions and standards around me say. In fact, at the time I am writing this paragraph I am 37 years old. In a few of the groups of women trying to conceive that I follow, I see more 30- and 40-year-old women trying to conceive their first child. Wherever we are in our journey, God sees us. It's not too late. Time is certainly not up. God will have His perfect way. It's easy in our current day to grow impatient in the waiting, but we have to remember that God is not bound by time and our concept of time is completely different from His.

From our perspective, time is running out.

From His, time never ends.

"Hope deferred maketh the heart sick: but when the desire cometh, it is a tree of life."

Proverbs 13:1

6

A Willingness to Do Anything

Jacob, Rebekah's second born twin, matured and had his own encounter with the God of Abraham who promised that his seed would be as the dust of the earth. Try counting that! Another promise of fruitfulness is spoken from the mouth of a God that had not failed yet! Surely, he had heard of how his father, Isaac, was the promised son of a barren woman, and how even he was one of the miracles that opened his own barren mother's womb.

Prior to embarking on this journey where he would encounter God, his father blessed him and sent him on his way to find a wife of his kindred, saying "God Almighty bless thee, and make thee fruitful, and multiply thee, that thou mayest be a multitude of people" (Genesis 28:3-4). His father prayed, "God bless thee" and God responded, "You will be blessed." Jacob had no idea he was going to be the third generation in his family to deal with barrenness. This journey is one that no one wants. It's a badge of honor only truly celebrated at the conclusion of it.

But God knew.

He sees every area of our lives. And what we think is a mistake, disaster, or an impossible situation, He looks upon it and says, "that's perfect! This is precisely what I'm looking for. I can use this!"

In the end, He will get the glory.

Rebekah and Rachel's stories were very similar in more ways than one. Jacob, too, had found a woman at a well and she also would be the vessel chosen to show God's glory and miraculous power. However, an older sister remained unmarried and, according to custom, she should have been given the opportunity to marry first. But Rachel was the one Jacob desired for his wife. After what I can only imagine being a lengthy discussion on the matter, Jacob agreed to serve Laban, his future father-in-law, for seven years in exchange for the hand of his beloved Rachel as his wife. The passage from Genesis 29:20 captures the sentiment that "they seemed to him but a few days." In other words, Rachel was worth the wait. It may sound cliche, but when it's God's will, His timing will be perfect, no matter how long it seems.

Your promise is worth the wait!

When the time finally came for Jacob to receive his bride, he was tricked by his father-in-law who snuck Leah into the marriage bed instead of Rachel. As a result, Jacob vowed to work another period of time for the right sister. Seeing that Leah as favored less than Rachel, God "opened her womb." To make the matter even more burdensome, Rachel was barren.

I can hear Rachel crying out to God: "You know how much I want this, Lord. I waited several years for this! This was not supposed to happen. It's so unfair!"

The Bible gives no reason to believe that Leah couldn't bear on her own. It's only mentioned that God opened her womb. I am not an expert Bible scholar, but my interpretation and understanding of this passage is that it's a great possibility Leah's body functioned appropriately and cycled through the natural processes of fertility the way God had created in the beginning. One translation of this verse states God made her "fertile" because she was being neglected as a wife (Genesis 29:31 ISV). Ladies who are trying to conceive understand the process of tracking ovulation on a calendar or chart. They are well aware of the narrow window of time each month known as the fertile period, curing which conception is most likely to occur. If your husband just isn't interested or is acting out of pure duty – likely as little as he can get away with, the probability of hitting that specific timeframe is very slim. Leah wasn't the wife Jacob wanted, and this may have very well been the case. Again, scripture doesn't specifically give us these details, and this is just speculation on my part, but it may have been that God sped up the "biological clock" so to speak and caused her to be fertile in that moment so she would conceive right at that time.

Rachel, however, is specifically labeled as barren, meaning of surety she had a breakdown in her body's natural reproductive processes that hindered her from conceiving.

For Leah, it could have potentially happened, but God chose to intervene to cause it to happen in His timing.

For Rachel, it wasn't going to happen <u>until</u> God intervened.

Unlike Sarah, who made the decision to involve another woman in her marriage, Rachel found herself in a situation where she had no control. She was the chosen bride, but her father tricked the man she was preparing to marry into marrying her older sister instead. Despite the betrayal, Jacob remained committed to Rachel and patiently waited for her. Rachel endured a period of time during which her sister occupied the marriage bed made for her.

Can you imagine her pain? Rachel's day finally comes to marry her man and her sister is conceiving his child. And then she conceived again, and again, and again. Imagine what Rachel must have thought:

"Will it ever be my turn?"

"She can have four children, but can I just have one, Lord?"

What agony she must have felt. Granted, her situation is extreme with the sister in the picture, but we are living in a world where affairs do happen, and it's a high probability that there is someone reading this story right now considering how it remotely resembles their own. Regardless of this extreme circumstance, have you ever had a thought like this when those around you are getting pregnant so easily? I can't say a thought like that hasn't ever crossed my mind. It's highly unlikely it never crossed hers.

These women listed throughout scripture were just ordinary women like the rest of us. Yet God just chose them to have extraordinary stories, just like me and you! We can take comfort knowing the God of all power who worked it out for their good can work it out for ours as well. Our stories aren't finished yet. The ending is still being written.

Remember that definition of desire? It can be so strong that it influences our will and drives us into action, even if those actions are inappropriate or against the will of God. The longer time goes by without it being fulfilled, the more we may be willing to consider doing for it. We can become irrational in our thinking and if we're not careful, we can cross our own boundaries. Rachel did just that! She saw her sister with her fourth child by her husband and she is childless. Of course, she desired to mother a child. She was a woman. It was something she longed for. So, she goes to her husband and demands, "Give me children or else I die" (Genesis 30:1).

She was grieving.

"I can't take this anymore. This is literally killing me. I don't think I can survive another cycle without conceiving. I cannot bear this any longer."
I've been there.

On top of the agonizing grief she experienced, there was strife, jealousy, and bitterness in her heart for her sister. There was another woman in her husband's tent who was bearing him children while she could not. So, she demands children of her husband who in return rebukes her telling her that only God can fulfill that request. "Am I in God's stead, who hath withheld from thee the fruit of the womb?" (Genesis 30:2). I'm sure this felt like rejection. Not to mention that God could have intervened on Rachel's behalf just as He did for Leah. But He hadn't.

. . . yet.

Just because He could have and didn't, doesn't mean He failed. There was a purpose for her pain.

Oh, what a message there is in this! I don't know how many things I've thought I desperately needed that God could have done but didn't. I suppose I will know on the other side of eternity, but rest assured, God is still so good to me. He has never failed.

Rachel knew what the Almighty God could do. Surely, Jacob told her of how he was the miracle that opened his mother's barren womb, and that God had provided as He said He would. She likely even knew of Sarah's testimony.

The descendants of Abraham's son through Sarah's servant girl were still roaming around in Rachel's neck of the woods. In the biblical narrative, Joseph, Rachel's son, would eventually be sold to these relatives by his own brothers. Surely, she knew great uncle Ishmael and Grandpa Isaac had some conflict and probably even knew the gritty details of that family drama. It is written in the Bible and Moses, the man that allowed God to use his hand to write this biblical account lived a few hundred years later. If he heard the story, Rachel had also heard it. But instead of finding comfort in her God, knowing that what He did once He can do again, even for her, what did she choose to do?

She crossed her own boundaries.

She couldn't stand that her sister could conceive her husband's children when she couldn't. In a desperate attempt to rectify the situation herself, she gave her husband her servant. Again, *another* woman bore her husband's children and the thermostat on that sibling rivalry cranked up a few more notches. It became a battle over who could have more children as

Leah also included her handmaid in the game. It is beyond my understanding why Jacob allowed this to continue, but certainly no one's focus was on the Lord. They trusted in their own devices and allowed desire and the lusts of the flesh to once again step in the way of promise.

This shows that strong desires will drive us to great lengths to achieve what we set our hearts on, no matter what the cost. It's a beast that when left untamed can destroy everything in its path. What they failed to remember is that God had a plan, and that plan was spoken. Our ways often end in pain and disappointment. We often try so hard to keep control when our Heavenly Father really just needs us to surrender that control so His perfect will can be done. He can't drive if our hands are clenching the steering wheel. Instead of making a way, we are often getting *in the way*.

Thankfully, we serve a merciful God.

Three ladies in this family had no idea God had a plan for them bigger than what they could even think or imagine, especially when the world told them it was impossible. Many mighty men of God came from wombs touched by the hand of God Almighty, not by their back-up plans or their futile attempts to find the will of God. He is fighting for us but will not stop us from trying to fight our own battles our way. We often feel we need to be doing something in the waiting but let me just say that waiting on God is not synonymous with being idle or doing nothing. On the contrary, it is *very* hard work. The Bible calls this longsuffering. If we can find a place in this season to sit and wait, trust in Him, and draw closer to Him so that we can feel the leading of His spirit, we can trust that His Word will come to pass in His way and in His timing. And oh, what a sweet day of rejoicing that will be!

"Wait on the LORD: be of good courage, and he shall strengthen thine heart: wait, I say, on the LORD.

Psalms 27:14

7

Seeking His Truth

My husband and I moved across the country from the east coast to Alaska in December 2016. Neither of us were living for God at the time. I grew up in a little church in the middle of nowhere. What a sweet little place that was as I think back on my childhood. It was a 100-year-old church that had a bell I loved to ring. There weren't many other kids in that little congregation, so I didn't have much competition. As I grew to be a teenager, my priorities quickly changed. I had never developed a true relationship with the Lord. Church was something I could choose, and although I enjoyed it, the things of this world caught ahold of me.

I had just turned 31 when we came to Alaska. We had no children, just a few dogs that we left back home with some friends to care for while we were away for this trip. I was a travel nurse, and this was supposed to be a three-month stint, however we quickly decided we wanted to stay for longer. Alaska has its way of doing that to you. Its beauty and mystery draws you. We also strongly believe it was the will of God for our lives to be here and He has given us a burden for this area.

It was -50°F that winter, and in case you weren't aware, winters here are *dark*. Everyone raved about how beautiful it was here in the summer and, of course, the sun never went down for a period of time, so we decided to extend our contract through July just to experience the other side of the extreme.

    Before coming to Alaska, I was in a really dark place mentally and emotionally and I was completely lost spiritually. Secretly, I wanted to go back to church, and even made promises to go when I would be invited to church by one of my friends. I attempted to keep those promises time after time, but sadly when the day came, I made some excuse as to why I wouldn't go. Usually, it was that I didn't feel well and chose to sleep in instead. I had some health issues I didn't fully understand at the time, so this wasn't completely a lie. I really didn't feel well and initially my motives truly were sincere. But the lifestyle and recreational choices I made played a big part in how bad I felt come Sunday morning. Honestly, at this point in my life, I just hadn't made church attendance, or any other spiritual disciple for that matter, a priority. Thankfully, some events took place that drove me to the Sanctuary UPC in Fairbanks where I found myself right in the arms of Jesus. I completely surrendered my life to Him, started reading the Bible, and completed it on my thirty-second birthday. It was the best gift I could have given myself, and I remember the extreme sense of accomplishment I felt as I pulled out my bookmark, sat it aside, and closed my Bible. It took me around seven months to finish reading it which completely astounds me. I always wanted to read the Bible through in a year before but could never find the motivation or momentum. The baptism of the Holy Ghost completely changed this for me, and I was completely in love and on fire for the Lord with an insatiable spiritual hunger to know everything, as much as He would reveal to me.

    One night, I was sitting at my table reading the word of God. I worked twelve-hour shifts in the emergency department then and my shifts often went into the night. Because of this, I was usually awake much later than my husband and I would often pray and read in the stillness of the midnight hours. On this night, I was reading in Judges, a book of the Bible I had never read before. I opened my Bible to where my bookmark was and started my nightly reading. I previously read about Sarah, Rebekah, and Rachel, and knew their testimonies. While all of these women's stories had a profound impact on my life, there's a sweet, sweet place in my heart for this woman I am about to introduce– and I don't even know her name.

At this moment in biblical history, the children of Israel had relapsed into idolatry and the enemy invaded the promised land. They were governed by a series of judges and had no official king, other than the One they turned their backs on of course: the King of Kings, our great and mighty God. The Israelites had been in a vicious cycle of sinning, repenting, going to battle with the enemy, and being delivered by the victorious hand of God, just for them to stumble into sinning again. Due to their constant falling away, God delivered them into the hands of the Philistines, a neighboring nation, for a period of forty years. A man named Manoah (which in the Hebrew means "Rest") had a wife who bears no name, and she was barren (Judges 13:2). Just like those before her, God had a plan, and she had no idea her son would be one of the mighty men God would use to deliver His people from their captivity.

As I read Judges 13 for the very first time, I wondered if God could move on my behalf, especially during my battle with infertility. We struggled to get pregnant for nearly nine years at this point. My health was not in a great place and the doctors said that it would be almost impossible for me to get pregnant naturally without medical intervention.

Here's a little back story. Shortly after our marriage, during a period when my husband and I were in two different states for a few months, I decided to look into my reproductive health. As I previously mentioned, neither of us had been living for God. Regrettably, we were in an intimate relationship without taking any protective measures before marriage for about three years and we already knew that we had a difficult time getting pregnant. While my husband was away, I decided to investigate why it had been so difficult.

My OBGYN referred me to a reproductive endocrinologist who

ordered a vast array of diagnostic testing: a DEXA scan to check on my bone structure and health to ensure I could carry a baby to term, an MRI of my pituitary and brain to ensure I didn't have a pituitary tumor, and a hysterosalpingogram (HSG) to ensure there were no blockages in my fallopian tubes. On top of all the studies and scans, I had ultrasounds checking my ovaries, uterus, and cervix, and a ton of blood work.

The results showed that both of my fallopian tubes were open, my uterus was small and slightly tilted but of no concern, and most of the other ultrasounds came back unconcerning. However, the MRI showed that my pituitary was not well formed, and I was diagnosed with Empty Sella Syndrome as well as human growth hormone deficiency, and the blood work showed that all of my reproductive hormones were nearly non-existent. A later more definitive diagnosis revealed that I had a congenital defect in a portion of my brain, as well as the pituitary gland, and my optic nerve; a rare condition called Septo-Optic Dysplasia. To receive this diagnosis, you must have at least two of those three things. I was very fortunate (sarcastically) to bear all three, and this condition affects more than just my reproductive organs; it affects my entire endocrine system.

My pituitary gland was not sending the signals to my ovaries and uterus to respond in an appropriate way for my ovaries to mature an egg and release it in ovulation or to ensure my uterine lining was thick enough for implantation should conception occur. This shed some light on why I did not have a menstrual cycle more than a slim handful of times a year, at most, since puberty began. We knew there were challenges ahead.

Our reproductive endocrinologist started me on a ton of medication. About a year later, we tried medicated cycles with injections to cause me to ovulate in an attempt for pregnancy along with timed intercourse. My body responded beautifully on the first cycle with medication and treatment. There were several mature follicles on my ovaries, and I had actually ovulated. To my discouragement, it did not result in pregnancy. We spent over $1000 just on medication, and I had to go every other day for blood work as well as a few scattered ultrasounds in the days surrounding injections and ovulation to see how my body progressed with treatment. This was not a cheap treatment option.

We decided to go for round two the following month, but my body did not respond as well this time. If I remember correctly, it was around twenty-eight days of trying to get any of the eggs in my ovaries to mature. For context, this occurs within just a few days for a woman with a healthy, regular cycle. I ended up in the emergency room one morning with stroke-like symptoms; my entire left side was numb, and my speech was slurred so badly that no one could understand what I was saying. It turned out that my thyroid had crashed as well as my adrenal glands, which meant I started on more medication. Thankfully, these conditions resolved as soon as I stopped the treatment and I soon recovered. It was too much for my already fragile endocrine system to handle; we were pushing my body too hard. This second cycle was around $2800 just in medication, not including the blood work, the ultrasounds, and the emergency room visit.

My husband did not want to go further, and I was honestly afraid to take more of the medication. I worried about how my body would respond. We decided to stop trying in that manner. Although it brought some relief from the fear concerning my health as well as the financial burden, I was devastated!

Remember that definition of desire in chapter 5? I was willing to do ANYTHING! Moving forward to IVF was not a possibility for us in that time of life as it would consist of similar hormones that would likely result in similar issues with my health. Looking back now, I'm thankful we didn't go that far. I couldn't bear the thought of having several embryos, living cells with both my husband's and my own DNA which are essentially the beginning stages of an unborn baby living in a dish somewhere waiting to be used or discarded – not to mention the thought of *how* they'd be discarded.

This thought just doesn't sit well with me spiritually.

The thought of using donor eggs or a surrogate was heart wrenching for me. I desired to conceive a child with my husband, carry it to term, and deliver it. I wanted the full experience I knew my body was made for. It felt hopeless, but I had no idea that God had a bigger plan for us. Medical science is a wonderful thing that I believe God allows in certain circumstances, but if it's not His timing, it's just not time.

A year or two later God led us to Alaska, and I started reading the Bible for the very first time. I didn't understand how to wait on God or even that God was trustworthy enough to wait on, honestly. As I said previously, I lacked a *relationship* with Him. He knew me but I didn't really know Him.

As soon as I came to Alaska, God started dealing with me about my health, and I found a clean version of the ketogenic diet. I'm not advocating for this way of eating or to trying to convince you that it will work for you. I believe you should prayerfully consider any change to your eating habits as some things can be detrimental to some people, but this is my story and without explaining this piece, the remainder of the significance of Manoah's wife's story to my own will be lost. I also started going to a gym in town and running on the treadmill, weighing myself, and counting carbohydrates. It wasn't long before I started losing weight and eventually even had a menstrual cycle without medication. This was liberating! I learned that my previous way of eating was causing inflammation, and following a low-fat diet was restricting the way my body metabolized these hormones, some of which actually require cholesterol.

In my studies of infertility, it's evident that nutrition is extremely important. Think about the condition of the garden and the food sources there that were in pristine condition in the beginning of Creation. Our modern-day diets are nutritionally lacking in many vital minerals and nutrients, but it wasn't always this way. Most conventional medicine practitioners agree that pregnant women and even women striving to become pregnant should take prenatal vitamins due to the affects nutritional deficiencies can have on the mother and the baby very early in pregnancy. The food we eat alone doesn't provide the nutrients to prevent them from occurring and almost everyone will agree this is true.

One thing that was not commonly spoken about in the conventional medicine world but is becoming more widely studied as people are becoming sicker and sicker is the power of inflammation. There are many clinical studies that show elevated levels of inflammatory markers present in many, if not all, of the top causes for infertility such as polycystic ovarian syndrome (PCOS), endometriosis, premature ovarian failure, and even unexplained infertility.

Inflammation is a natural and healthy response that keeps the body in balance, working the way God designed it. However, when the trigger to the inflammatory response is not removed from the equation, the body is never able to finish the inflammatory process and inflammation becomes chronic or long-lasting. Chronic inflammation leads to "dis-ease" in the body. Take a guess as to what the top causes of inflammation are apart from injury. If you guessed anything in the food category, you are correct. Second and potentially even tied in first place is stress, something we know an awful lot about these days.

A quick internet search will reveal a handful of ways to reduce inflammation and almost all of the strategies you'll find include food choices and stress management. God cares about the things we put into our mouths so much that He included prohibitions for eating certain things in the Old Testament law. Not to mention the fact that the only restriction in the garden was not to eat the fruit of a single tree. God set strict boundaries on what is clean and unclean, and His chosen people were to separate themselves from all uncleanness. It wasn't just for identity, signifying a people who were dedicating themselves to a holy God, but considering the food preparation in their day, things like shellfish and pork may have potential adverse effects on their health if not cooked in a thorough manner.

Some things throughout scripture are listed as an abomination to God and some are listed as an abomination to us. These things will not serve us well if we choose to partake. Our choices are incredibly significant to God, including our choice of food.
Fast forward a few thousand years, our modern-day diets are full

of processed and refined foods that increase inflammatory markers, lead to obesity, and ultimately disease and death. In Genesis, God said everything He made was good but out of convenience we have chosen to alter it. I find it interesting that in His promise in Exodus and Deuteronomy, which we spoke of in a previous chapter, God promises protection from the illnesses of Egypt, representing the bondage of the world. He promised to bless their food and water, and – get this - nothing will suffer miscarriage or infertility, as long as they don't get entangled in the bondage of the world, serve their idols, and do their works. Our world today is in bondage to convenience!

I want to make it very clear that I do not believe that barrenness is in any way our fault or related to sin that we have committed or are committing in our lives. I do believe, however, that we are temples of His Spirit. Our bodies are a living sacrifice. We were bought with price, and we should feel compelled to do our part to be a good steward of the bodies He has entrusted in our care.

There are a ton of journal articles that are evidence-based and peer reviewed on the effects of food on fertility, including which supplements and lifestyle changes have been clinically trialed. I encourage you to do your research on any medical label that has been applied to you to see what you can do to improve your overall health and fertility. It was quite an eye-opening endeavor for me, and I'm still a work in progress. Fasting has been instrumental, mingled with a ton of prayer. These two things above all else have drastically impacted my health, and even more so my faith and relationship with Him!

In addition to my research on food and lifestyle choices, I completely stopped taking medication when I moved to Alaska. This was not intentional. After multiple attempts of trial and error, I could not get in contact with my doctor back home and the only endocrinologist in 350 miles would not see me unless I had records from my previous provider who had retired. The answering service to the other endocrinologist I saw back home never returned my call.

The menstrual cycle that occurred after drastically changing my diet sparked a new wave of hope within me, but it also came with sadness. It was still very irregular in occurrence, and I knew my health history. At the time, given my age and experiences to date, the situation seemed irreparable. I knew Jesus was able to heal others, and now that I had a relationship with Him, I had complete faith in His undeniable ability to do so. Yet somehow my situation still seemed impossible, even for our Mighty God. It was me. This was a perfect example of "Lord I believe, but help my unbelief."

I was just learning of Him and really, who was I in the span of His entire kingdom? From my perspective I was just a nobody from nowhere doing nothing seemingly significant for His kingdom, other than trying my best to be a faithful saint in that season. I used to tell people that I was hanging by a thread at the hem of His garment, white-knuckling it sometimes, clinging for dear life. All it takes to grab our God's attention is faith and faithfulness. It doesn't matter if you have major accomplishments in ministry or if others know your name. All that matters is that *He* knows your name!

"But seek ye first the kingdom of God, and his righteousness; and all these things shall be added unto you."

Matthew 6:33

8

Thou Shall Conceive a Son

Just as He spoke in the beginning and it simply was, God had a word that was just for me. This word would breathe life into dry bones and birth promise in circumstances that seemed hopeless, even impossible. Little did I know, this word of hope and peace that He would speak would be found as I navigated through the pages of the Word of God that contained Manoah's wife's story.

I remember it like it was yesterday. I flipped my Bible open to Judges 13, not realizing that God was about to speak to me in a very clear way or that my entire life was about to change. As I read through the scriptures, this got my attention:

"And the angel of the LORD appeared unto the woman, and said unto her, Behold now, thou art barren, and bearest not: but thou shalt conceive, and bear a son. Now therefore beware, I pray thee, and drink not wine nor strong drink, and eat not any unclean thing: For, lo, thou shalt conceive, and bear a son; and no razor shall come on his head: for the child shall be a Nazarite unto God from the womb: and he shall begin to deliver Israel out of the hand of the Philistines" (Judges 13:3-5)

The woman was barren. There was a promise spoken and she was directed to take action. She had a choice. Would she be obedient and accept this promise? I don't want to impose guilt upon any heart reading this; however, it's not uncommon for God to call us into action saying, "If you will, then I will."

God began to speak to me about eating and drinking appropriately, and He had shown me through my food choices that I had increasingly more energy and felt better when I ate the way He led me to eat. I had significantly less energy and felt horrible when I ate things that were not according to His plan for me. So here is a woman who was barren, and God told her, "You're going to conceive. Don't eat anything unclean." After studying this for several years, I know now that this passage of scripture tells a very deep story of consecration – the separation from unclean to clean, or holy. In that moment, though, it was a simple command from God. "Beware" and "eat not any unclean thing" (Judges 13:4).

Unclean in Manoah's wife's day was laid out in Leviticus and was much simpler than it is in our day. Today, we have genetically modified ingredients that our bodies have no idea how to digest, as well as many synthetic and man-made ingredients that are equally as difficult. All of these ultra-processed foods lead to inflammation in the body which we have previously established leads to infertility among other various forms of disease. I challenge you to try to find one food in the market today other than raw fruits, vegetables, and fresh meats that have no form of added sugar, a sugar substitute, or even any form of "natural" sugar. It's almost impossible! High fructose corn syrup and modified food starch, among others, are staples in the food industry today, not to mention genetically modified grains, soy, and corn. These items are often first ingredient on many food labels in our pantries. God showed me that I am a temple of His Holy Spirit and the things I *choose* to put into my body can be a blessing or a curse.

Judges 13:6 states "Then [after the conversation with the messenger of the Lord] the woman came and told her husband" all that he had spoken. My husband was not living for God at that time. I made the choice to come wholeheartedly back to church, but he had not. It was well after midnight, probably closer to two or three in the morning when I read that sentence, and I felt a strong urge to run to tell him what God had told me. I got up from that table and ran to the back bedroom where he slept, tapped him on the shoulder, and once he was startled awake, I said something like ,"I know you're not going to believe me, but God just told me that I was going to conceive a son." Of course, he was not enthused about being awakened, especially to hear what the Lord had said, but I needed to proclaim my faith , and I knew that if I kept this only in my heart, I would not have anyone to testify with me when it came to pass. I also felt I needed to speak it out loud to proclaim my faith. We are created in the image of God. When He speaks, things begin to happen. We are no different. Our words are powerful.

I'd had enough encounters with God at this point that I knew this was no coincidence. I lived this scripture, and I would be forever connected with this courageous woman with no name. In fact, during my weakest moments, God used her story to bring me encouragement and to keep me walking along the path He planned for me.

Manoah's wife ran to tell her husband all the Angel of the Lord said. When Manoah heard it, he asked the Lord to send the man of God who came to bear those good tidings once more so that he could tell them how to care for the child that would be born. He had great faith! He didn't doubt his wife's words. This couple knew and feared God. Although the children of Israel were led astray by false doctrines and succumbed to worshiping false idols, Manoah and his wife stayed faithful to their God. As a result, they found favor in the sight of the Lord. Without such a relationship, how else could they have had such trust and expectation in what was spoken over them?

Faithful as always, God answered that prayer, and the angel of the Lord came again to Manoah's wife. She ran to get her husband and he asked, "What shall we do with the child?" He responded, "of the things I told her, let her beware." This had to be a mutual agreement. Manoah's wife had to be consecrated, set apart from everyone else, because the child she would conceive needed to be consecrated from the womb and set apart for the plan God had for him. He could not be tainted by anything unclean in the world. God wanted a clean vessel.

The command to Manoah was simply, "Let her."

Lifestyle changes are significantly difficult, especially when no one else is on board with it. Have you ever tried to cut things out of your diet like cake, cookies, or chips, only to find your spouse going to town on a bag of your favorite Doritos? Lifestyle changes can also cost more family resources. This is definitely true in our day. Fresh fruits and vegetables are sometimes more expensive than canned or frozen options, and they spoil much quicker if they're not used in a timely manner.

Manoah's wife was a mighty woman of God and needed to submit to her husband if he disagreed with her choices. But God commanded him: "Let her."

Matthew Henry's commentary on this chapter of Judges describes how God often meets women in their season of most need. I am so thankful He met me in those seasons and continues to meet me still! Manoah's wife likely felt just as I did about her inability to have a child. She didn't have modern technology or medical science to tell her just where her body was failing, but what she did have was a promise from God. If she followed through on her end of the deal, her child would be a Nazarite from the womb, consecrated to the Master's use. He later delivered the Israelites from the hands of the Philistines.

Matthew Henry goes on to state that "many eminent persons were born of mothers that had been kept a great while in the want of the blessing of children, that the *mercy* might be more acceptable when it *did* come. Mercies long waited for often prove signal mercies, and it is made to appear that they are worth waiting for, and by them others may be encouraged to continue their hope in God's mercy."

Praise God! I find encouragement in these long seasons of waiting that I read about in the Word of God. It gives me hope!

If there was not a nameless barren woman married to a man named Manoah, there would not be a Samson. If there had been no Samson (or promised child to this barren couple), there would have been many seasons of my own life without a direct word from God. I can't even imagine how dark those seasons would have seemed. If it weren't for these women, I would not have the faith or hope to continue waiting and standing on the Word of God. This book, intended to be an encouragement to you of God's faithfulness and mercy in your own season of waiting, would never come to fruition.

"Thou hast turned for me my mourning into dancing: thou hast put off my sackcloth, and girded me with gladness."
Psalms 30:11

9

A Documented Miracle

It was a service like any other, and I had previously gone to the front for the elders of our church to anoint me with oil and lay hands on me several times in the past. We had just come out of a month-long church-wide season of prayer and fasting. I find it noteworthy that Jesus does not leave room to debate if fasting is expected of us; He simply declares "when you fast" (Matthew 6:16-18). I can testify that when we fast the way He tells us to in His Word (see also Isaiah 58), things happen (Mark 9:29).

During this service, our associate pastor interrupted the scheduled flow to proclaim he felt in the spirit that someone needed a miracle. I remained standing at my seat. Secretly, I felt an intense urge to go to the front; it was an urge so strong within me that gripped at my heart – you know, that internal check you feel within yourself that says, "You better listen!" Except it's not coming from your mom, but from God Himself!

Okay, it wasn't quite that dramatic, but I knew it was from the Lord and I knew I needed (and wanted) to be obedient.

Needless to say, I found myself standing at the altar. Much to my surprise, my husband was standing behind me. One of the ministers anointed me with oil and asked what I needed. I was shocked that I said my husband and I were trying to have a baby. Previously, unless it was a close female friend with whom I could openly be vulnerable with, I requested prayer for a healing of my medical condition and leave out the part about infertility. He prayed for us, and my faith rose a little, especially since the service was interrupted for this prayer request. As I mentioned before, I frequently requested prayer for this issue. Each time this happens a part of me worries that it will be like any other time. As time passes, my faith dwindles.

The next day, my phone rang.

The call was from a medical office I visited a few months prior for a wellness exam. I had new insurance and there was no out-of-pocket expense for that visit. I was taking charge of my health, so why not take advantage of this opportunity? Not to mention the Lord had me on this journey of healing (spiritually and physically). During that visit, I disclosed my previous diagnosis which I had been told would likely require lifelong medication; medication that I no longer took. I was not able to get an appointment to see the only endocrinologist in 350 miles.

The medical staff called to inform me that the endocrinologist wanted to see me [finally], but I needed to complete an MRI and some blood work first. It seemed a little odd to me that a provider would order tests to be completed before he actually saw me, but remembering what had just happened at church the day before, I scheduled the blood work for the next day. Before she drew my blood, I told the lab tech I needed to see the labels with my name placed on the tubes and watch as blood from my body was transferred into them. I'm sure she thought this was a strange request, but I didn't care. My faith was rising. In the event something miraculous did take place, I wanted to know with certainty that it was my blood in those tubes labeled with my name. I am a nurse and know that mistakes do happen, so I couldn't leave any room for error in this. I also didn't want to give doubt an opportunity to show its ugly face to steal my joy and cause me to believe God hadn't done what I know He did. I needed validation in my mind that the results would definitely be my own so that I could arrest those negative thoughts when they did come.

The lab tech informed me that some of the tests needed to be sent out of state for processing, which meant that it would be a week or more before I should expect to receive the results. Not expecting anything back any time soon, I went about life as usual.

Two days later, I got a call from the doctor's office again. I couldn't answer the call right away and it was forwarded to voicemail. I attempted to call back but was only able to leave a message. It was a dreadful game of phone tag. The next day, I received another call while I was sleeping. I worked weird hours and I often slept until the middle of the afternoon. When I woke and realized I had several messages from the doctor's office, I called them back immediately. I knew that all of my levels were nonexistent previously and that it might be concerning to someone who didn't know my history. My previous diagnosis was a birth defect, so I'd been this way my whole life; I was thirty-four when awaited these results. I also just wanted to know. The person who answered the phone asked me to leave a message for the provider once again, which admittedly caused me an incredible amount of frustration. I informed her of the urgency of the calls I received, as there were several voicemails, and that I was expecting my lab results to be significantly abnormal, which likely caused her concern. It was the end of the business day on a Friday, and I didn't want to wait until after the weekend to have this discussion. I urged her to allow me to speak with the provider.

After a long hold, she came back and said, "The provider wants me to tell you that your lab results are normal."

"Normal?" I thought. "They've never EVER been normal?!"

"Are you sure?" I was shocked.

I once heard someone say, "We should not be astounded when God does something, we should be astounded when He doesn't." He is a miracle-working God. Yet still, there was that thorn in my flesh I'd grown way too acquainted with: unbelief. Not the absence of belief that He *could*, but that He *would for me*.

I asked her to check again by looking at my actual lab results. She confirmed they were all normal except for the insulin-like Growth Factor-1 (IGF-1). This was the one I wanted to see the most and the medical office had not received the result. Previously, it was 18. A normal adult my age would have a level around 200, therefore a level of 18 was basically nonexistent.

She assured me once again that the levels were all normal, so I did what any unbelieving medical professional would do. I asked for the values of every lab test with results; then, I called my friends in the hospital lab. Working in the emergency department helped me develop some close contacts in that department, and thankfully one answered. I told her that I had some lab values and I needed to know the normal ranges for each test. I didn't tell her these were my results. She likely thought nothing of it. She had no idea if I was working or not and it wasn't abnormal for us to discuss patients' results.

Every lab value I wrote down was in normal range.

I didn't know this at the time, but the doctor's office that ordered the tests used the hospital lab, so the range considered normal would have been the same at either place. Some of those values were low normal, and some were high normal. But ALL were NORMAL! It was a documented miracle, and it was for *me*!

When I got the call from central scheduling to set up an appointment for the MRI, the technician informed me that my insurance denied the pre-authorization for treatment. Therefore, I needed to pay out of pocket for the test. They would not authorize the MRI because my lab work showed it was not necessary. It was a special scan of the pituitary gland, and the insurance company wanted some verification that there was an issue with this gland before shoveling out the money for it. With all of my pituitary hormones in the normal range, there was no medical necessity to jump straight into this test. In the eyes of my insurance company, the endocrinologist could not verify there was a problem. This was another documented miracle!

The IGF-1 had not come back yet, and I felt a little fear creep into my heart. What if it's not normal? I felt the peace of God in that moment and decided that I would not even call back for that level. Was I going to allow one value to cancel this miracle in my mind? God wanted me to trust in Him. In that moment I peacefully obeyed, and in faith I received that miracle without that value.

They never called to discuss the results of that last test. It was a month or so later that I felt the urge to log into the patient portal just to see. Deep inside I knew I should have just trusted and continued in my faith, but I wanted to know. And guess what? It was normal! That was the grace of God. He didn't change His mind because I caved in. When Peter walked on the water and fear began to grip his heart, Jesus didn't look at him and say, "well you didn't trust in me, so figure it out yourself." No. He grabbed his hand and held him up. I did such a happy dance at the sight of those results! Soon after that, my menstrual cycle returned again for one month. It was another sign that something indeed changed in my body. God was doing something for me, and I was beyond grateful.

A few months later we attended a district camp meeting. I had just surrendered the ideas I had to take things into my own hands. I let go of the idea of adoption, and God confirmed His plan by showing me Judges 13 a second time (see Chapter 3). This miracle had taken place; I had been healed. However—and that's just a fancy word for 'but…'—my menstrual cycle was still very irregular and seemingly non-existent, apart from the month after my healing took place. I leaned on my own understanding, and I couldn't help but think something was still not right.

"God, if you healed me, why isn't this problem fixed also? If I have normal hormone levels why isn't my body behaving like it?" I'm thankful the Lord really does enjoy it when we run to Him with all of our worries and fears. I know mine have to be very grievous sometimes.

Wanting answers, I went to our district camp meeting with an expectation for God to speak to me about His promise and what He was doing in my life. I needed some encouragement . . . even still.

I thought the entire camp meeting that I might be pregnant. I experienced some symptoms that were odd for me as most of my reproductive organs are pretty silent the majority of the time. I'd have never even known they were in there if I hadn't seen them on an ultrasound years ago. My faith had been restored and I knew it was possible. I asked Him to speak to me, so each day I was eagerly seeking and anticipating to hear His voice. During one of our day services, Bro. Marrell Cornwell preached on home Bible studies. In the middle of his sermon, seemingly out of nowhere, he changed pace and spoke of his gift of pregnancy. I completely misunderstood what he was speaking about and thought he was talking about birthing spiritual children, new converts. It was so out of place in that message. He described one of his ministries which includes praying for couples who have struggled with infertility. He reported that his previous success rate had been 100%, meaning God had given him favor in this area and acted on his prayer of faith. Again, it was completely out of the blue, but he asked for couples who experienced infertility to see him at the conclusion of the service for prayer.

Before I knew it, my husband was dragging me up to him. He looked at us with amazement. The service wasn't over! But why wait? There was such an expectation for God to move in that moment that he prayed for us right then. He led us into proclaiming a new marriage covenant with each other, which basically renewed our wedding vows right there in that service. It was a beautiful experience, and spiritually it brought healing to my heart. Our first few years of marriage were very rocky and would have been difficult even if we hadn't struggled with infertility. There were hurts and we were carrying around some emotional baggage. God knew what we needed more than anything in that service.

I'm not sure how accurate my memory is on this, but somehow in my mind, I perceived that he said everyone for whom he prayed conceived within three months. A one hundred percent success rate was a pretty good track record! Our camp meeting was in the last week of June, so by the end of September I was completely devastated that the promise hadn't come to pass. As we got close to the time I felt this promise should have been fulfilled, I thought within myself "God, I don't know what this will do to my faith if it doesn't happen." I had been in the church for two years and my husband for about a year. What a test of faith! Needless to say, it didn't happen in that timing. I hate to admit this, but I entered into a very dark period of questioning almost every word from God spoken by a human for a period of two to three years. I knew God was able for others, but I didn't know if He would come through in this for me, even though I know I heard Him speak to me and say that He would on more than one occasion.

In 2020, I was reading the Bible on a 90-day reading plan with a friend from church. We got to Judges 13 and I told her my story. Just prior to this, on the same day, I called my husband up in the middle of the night to proclaim faith in the promise of God. Here's my journal entry from that moment:

Journal Entry: 4/11/2020

I was in prayer, felt to wake Joey up to proclaim faith and call Heaven and Earth to record that we believe and receive this promise. Joey didn't want to get up to pray, so I went back to my room and finished praying. Then Jornie called to read, and it was Judges 13. I knew it was going to be Judges 13, so this wasn't unexpected, but after we finished reading and I told Jornie my testimony [the first time God spoke to me about Judges 13, and how I ran to tell Joey the promise of the Lord], it dawned on me that a similar event just took place. This is still a promise.

Manoah thought surely he would die because he saw the Lord, but his wife said not so because God had made her a promise that had not yet been fulfilled. My God made me a promise, and It shall come to pass!

It's so incredible that once again, during a dark season, God led me back to Judges 13, and He allowed me to relive an experience from three years prior. Unfortunately, the stress of working in a busy emergency department during COVID, my dark season of questioning God, not following any of the dietary principles He had led me to and switching to night shift had completely burnt out my adrenal glands and really my entire already strained endocrine system. I had my labs checked again. Of course, every one of those normal labs went right back in the toilet. I should have known better! Remember Lot's wife? God doesn't want us to look from where He brought us.

Two years later in 2022, I went to a baby shower. It was a friend of ours from church who had asked us to care for their child in the unfortunate event anything happened to both of them at the same time. My husband and I agreed, and we eagerly accepted the invitation to be a part of this child's life. We both attended that baby shower. The shower was a beautiful experience, but I became exhausted toward the end of it. I didn't feel sadness or grief while I was there, but I do remember becoming more withdrawn and internalized in my thoughts and actions. As we got in the truck and began to pull away, tears started streaming down my face. I was hurting tremendously and the flood gates to grief opened in an instant! My husband looked at me and asked what was wrong, but the only thing I could say was, "I'm just sad." That was the last baby shower I ever attended. The three-day period of grief that followed was agony, but I allowed myself to feel it. I needed to prove to myself that this truly was still my desire, and honestly, I needed something to snap me out of the spiritual rut I was in.

After three days, I called some ladies from church that I admired. Each of them spoke to me with incredible wisdom. One told me about a dietary plan her endocrinologist told her about. It was the same dietary plan my naturopath mentioned to me when I was seeking assistance with dietary guidelines to follow and was completely in line with what I researched regarding foods that affect fertility as well as with most of what God had shown me. I was struggling! I love baking and sweets, both of which are full of sugar and flour, and are incredibly high on the list of inflammatory foods. I learned that I find comfort in food. That's a problem because the only true Comforter is Jesus Christ, and nothing satisfies that void quite like He does! Judges 13 rang heavily in my ear. "Eat no unclean thing for you will conceive a son."

A few weeks after speaking with those incredible women of God, I heard Bro. Eli Hernandez preach on faith. He mentioned that he would pray for people to be healed, and they were. God honored that prayer, but on some occasions, the pain or specific ailment would return, and the person would ask him to pray again. He explained that it wasn't that they needed God to perform another miracle. God had done His part, and what God does He does well. The issue was fear. Fear cancels faith. Many times in the New Testament Jesus proclaims to the believer "your faith has made you whole." Bro. Hernandez prayed for their faith to be restored instead of God healing them again. His miraculous work had already been done, and it was up to them to receive it. When I heard this, I buckled down on the floor in a snotty crying mess. It knocked every bit of breath out of my lungs and sucker punched my heart. That was a blow I didn't see coming. I realized that I had let go of my faith in God's promise, and probably even His ability or desire to miraculously heal me, even though I had documented medical proof that He already had! I had an upper room experience in my loft bedroom that day, basking in the joy of the Lord.

My faith had been restored . . . again.

Since my health declined in 2020, I was back on all of those "lifelong" medications which included an injection that cost me over $80 a month. With supplements and meds, I paid about $300 every other month or so. I think it goes without saying that it was quite expensive. Several providers informed me that some of these medications I could not stop, or it could be life threatening. They had no idea I'd been toiling with the idea of quitting my medication since my upper room encounter a few weeks prior. I had been without them for years and God sustained me. I believed He was big enough to do it again. He's still God.

One night, I was walking up the stairs to my bedroom when I realized I hadn't taken my medication, especially my nighttime injection. I turned around to go back down and the Holy Ghost stopped me. Deep within me there was a stillness, and I felt at peace about not taking them. I decided to forget the medication for the time being and started back up the stairs toward my bed.

After that night, I decided to completely stop taking everything, and that I wouldn't mention it to anyone in case they'd disagree or worry. In fact, I was scared to death to go to my doctor's appointment because my endocrinologist was adamant that I would need some of these meds for the rest of my life. His passion for his patients' health and wellbeing often caused him to come off as very stern. Standing up for myself and keeping strong boundaries in my decisions had always been very difficult for me, so I was intimidated to disagree with him. Thankfully, the Lord worked that out. I canceled next appointment when I realized I'd be out of town for camp meeting. I never scheduled another one.

Our church in Fairbanks hosted our district ladies retreat a week or two later. Like I typically do when we have large church-related events, I went into this conference with an eager expectation to hear from God. Just like before, I wanted a rekindled promise.

I know what you might be thinking, "Again? She needs ANOTHER confirmation?"

Well... Yes.

You see, Gideon was a mighty man of God, and God had to confirm to him over and over that He was going to lead him in the victory over the enemy. But Gideon still had to "fleece" it. And when God revealed His ways, he had to fleece it again. Even still, after all of that, God had to take him to the enemy's camp so he could overhear his enemies discussing a dream one of them had about how Gideon's God would be on his side and deliver his enemies into his hand. God spoke to him repeatedly to convince him that He really would lead them to victory (see Judges 6:11 - 7:15). God knows our human weaknesses. So here I was, fleecing God for another confirmation of what He had spoken to me time and time again.

I hope you're feeling encouraged, friend.

I took the week of the conference off work and spent an hour or two each day at the church in prayer in a closet where no one could see me or hear me. My intention was that no one would even know I was there apart from my car outside, which I would have parked elsewhere if our church wasn't in such a rough part of town. We have a busy church with people there any time of day on any day of the week. It's difficult to get alone there with the Lord sometimes, but even in the hustle and bustle of preparing for ladies' retreat, I was able to find my hole in the wall to get alone with Him. I was desperate. I needed to tap into that unwavering and steadfast faith I once had that could move mountains, the faith the Word of God speaks of. I needed to clear the clutter out of my mind in the stillness of an old dusty cement room so that I could hear Him speak. By the time our ladies retreat started, my heart was fertile ground eagerly anticipating seeds to be planted.

Sis. Wanda Chavis spoke a message called "Waiting for Dreams to Come True" on the last evening service that Friday night. In that message, she said, "you heard from God. He made you a promise. He will make good on that promise." I know that word was for me. There was no question about it.

After service there was an altar call and one of our youth girls came to seek the Holy Ghost. As I prayed with her, an unknown woman whose voice I cannot place a name to came up behind me and started praying. I assumed she was praying for our youth girl as other ladies had gathered around us praying for her in that altar service. But this lady said, "You have heard the audible voice of God, you heard what she said." She repeated Sis. Chavis' statement that spoke to me. Something in me broke. It was so tangible that other women in that service felt it, too. One woman told me after service that God had spoken to her as she saw me praying off to the side and said He was going to give me my promise. The next morning after service another lady told me that God informed her He was going to answer my prayer. There was such an urgency she felt in the Spirit that she told me she felt I would get pregnant very soon.

The next day was Sunday, and during our regular church service, a friend walked up to me. As I began to tell her all God had done, she said "Sis, I didn't want to tell you because I didn't want to hurt your feelings, but I felt like God spoke to me and told me He was going to answer your prayer and give you that baby." Another friend right after that said the exact same thing. That was six people total, including Sis. Chavis! And not one of them knew what the others had said. I went home and threw those medications away so that I would NEVER be tempted to take them again. And I took a picture of my trash can heaping with medication to send to all those I trusted in the Lord for accountability. God spoke and I was not going to lose out on my hope of this promise again! I was sick and tired of allowing fear and my own stubborn impatience to cancel my faith!

And guess what! God is still sustaining me. I've since had repeated blood work that showed that all the results returned to normal. And it's all for His glory!

I wonder what would happen if you took a few moments to search your heart right now to see if your heart is fertile ground that can bring forth the fruit of your promise. Jesus said, "And all things, whatsoever we ask in prayer, believing, we shall receive" (Matthew 21:22). What would it take to rekindle a spark in your heart to give you the strength to stand on the Word of God in this season of waiting? When I say that I am no one special, I really mean it. And God is no respecter of persons. So, if He can speak a word of promise to me, I know He is eager to speak a word of promise to you! I know that the unknown seems scary, and the timing seems long, but if we can find a little bit of faith within us, we can draw out a little bit of hope, and He will give us the grace we need to keep standing a little longer. He is a promise keeper! If He gave you a promise, it will surely come to pass!

"Then shall thy light break forth as the morning, and thine health shall spring forth speedily: and thy righteousness shall go before thee; the glory of the LORD shall be thy rereward."

Isaiah 58:8

10

Entering Into the Secret Place

Psalm 46 begins "God is our refuge and strength, a very present help in trouble. Therefore, will not we fear, though the earth be removed, and though the mountains be carried into the midst of the sea; Though the waters thereof roar and be troubled, though the mountains shake with the swelling thereof. Selah" (Psalm 46:1-4).

Selah means to simply pause and reflect on what was spoken. When this word is used throughout scripture, it encourages us to pay close attention and meditate on what we have just read. What is this message really saying? What's the significance, the power?

This is one of my favorite chapters of the Bible. It speaks to me. It brings me comfort, encourages me, and leads me to a place of safety; safety from the winds of this life that blow any which way; safety from the emotional responses to trials, from the fiery darts of the evil of this world, and from the pressure to be conformed to a world that is not my home in which I try to navigate with garments as clean and white as snow. Imagine how difficult it is to keep anything white clean. We live in a fallen world, and it is sometimes an exhausting effort to prevent the stains of bitterness, covetousness, and fear, among others, from setting in.

The writer of this Psalm declares there is a secret place, a place of refuge and strength, no matter the circumstances we find ourselves in. Imagine a world in utter chaos where the ground beneath us literally shakes and caves in all around us as waters rise and rage across the land as they literally swallow up mountains, devouring anything else in its way. This picture that I envision when thinking of this world reminds me of an old apocalyptic or end-of-the-world type movie I watched as a child. There is turmoil everywhere we look. The writer encourages us that our God is our refuge and strength *even in that!*

I don't know about you, but this is what my fertility struggle has felt like to me. Despite this, I have learned that there is a place of stillness God has for me, and it's in His presence, alone, shut in, and shut off from the elements outside. This includes the expectations and perceptions that plague my thought life. This is what Bro. Ken Gurley refers to as the "trysting" place in his book *The Book on Prayer*. It's a place of intimacy with God, a place where I can bring the open wounds that I've tried to bandage and mend myself in my own ways, and I can uncover them, allowing myself to be completely vulnerable with God, and show Him my deepest most secret parts, so He can do what only He can do. It's a place of rawness and complete surrender. A place of holding nothing back. It's a place where we realize we are not enough, but He is more than enough. This place is *prayer* in its truest sense. It's the place where a broken and contrite spirit meets in sweet communion with a Holy and faithful God. Hannah knew about this place.

Hannah was an incredible intercessor who knew how to get God's attention and her story had an incredible impact on my own. Like Rachel, Hannah had no choice but to share her husband with another woman in the house. That other woman was able to bear her husband's children (see 1 Samuel 1:2,5). This grieved her tremendously, as it would any of us if we were in her situation. Peninnah taunted her year after year until one day it was too much for her to bear. The grief of her heart was so heavy that she could not eat (see 1 Samuel 1:7).

I know what that is like, sadly. I recently came out of a season of grief so heavy that any other amount of stress this world threw at me was too much for me to handle.

For several months, I had difficulty swallowing certain foods and even choked a few times. This instilled fear inside of me when I would try to eat anything. It grew incredibly worse after my miscarriage. The muscles in my face, neck, shoulders, chest, and even my diaphragm had become so tense that it literally made it impossible for me to eat anything that was not baby food consistency. For three weeks, I lived off protein shakes and pouches of pureed fruit. I began to even have difficulty swallowing Jello and applesauce, and I lost at least five pounds. It was such a dark time in my life that I had to be placed on short-term disability from work for a few weeks – and it was all the result of the intense stress of unresolved grief. Despite their sincere attempts, no one understood what I was going through, and everyone to whom I spoke about it seemed shocked that my symptoms were *only* stress. Although I know this is not true, at the time, I felt like those around me thought I was going insane, and I was starting to wonder if they were right. Stress wreaks havoc on your body.

Like no one could quite understand my grief, Hannah's husband did not understand hers either. He seemingly accepted the state of her womb, and wondered why Hannah was so distraught. After all, she had him. Was he not good enough for her? He already had sons and daughters by his other wife (1 Samuel 1:4) and Hannah was his prize (1 Samuel 1:5), so what more could he possibly ask for? From his perspective, life was pretty good, and he couldn't see a reason that Hannah wouldn't be content. But like the rest of us, Hannah's womb was meant to be fruitful, and that unfulfilled *desire* left a bitterness in her spirit that drove her right to this secret place.

Unresolved bitterness is like poison to our spirit and can cause us to be separated from the Lord if we don't deal with these emotions in an appropriate manner (Acts 8:21-23). Hannah knew exactly what she needed to do. She ran to the house of God, ripped the band aid off of her bleeding wounds, and cried out to her heavenly Father, "God, if You will look on my affliction - my pain, my stress, my grief - and if you'll see my faithfulness to You, and please remember me, and give me a son, I will give him to You all the days of his life, and he will be consecrated unto You for Your service, whatever You see fit!"

> "Daddy, I'm hurting. . .
> Look...
> See...
> Remember...
> I promise I'll surrender."

She pleaded with the Lord, bargaining with Him, saying, "If you will, Lord, I will." All she wanted was a chance to mother a child, and in return she was willing to sacrifice that child for the purpose of His Kingdom. As she poured every bit of herself out before the Lord, Eli the priest saw her praying silently in a way that only her lips moved. No one wants the world to hear our most intimate prayers. She held nothing back and the words she uttered were for the King of Kings alone. Eli couldn't hear a word she was saying. Because of this, he perceived she was drunk. He didn't understand her grief, either. In fact, he put his hands over her mouth and rebuked her (See 1 Samuel 1:11-14).

Hannah spoke up to the priest, saying "No, my lord, I am a woman of a sorrowful spirit and have poured out my soul before the Lord" (1 Samuel 1:15). She described her current state as an abundance of grief (1 Samuel 1:16). This pain she experienced was unrelenting, day in and day out, and grew more burdensome as time passed. She had an adversary at home who was flaunting her fertility. Hannah determined she was not going to leave until God moved in her situation. She was in such a place of desperation that it didn't matter what time it was, how long she'd spent in prayer, what her other obligations were in her busy life of routines and schedules. She was desperate to hear a word from God.

I listened to a powerful message recently by Bro. Jack Cunningham entitled "Understanding Prayer." The message was so very simple, yet profound. He said, "*all* you need is a word from God." It's that simple. It's everything we are searching for: a word from God. He reminded me in that simple message that "God said . . ." and it was. There was light, mountains, oceans, etc. Everything that exists in our natural world exists because God said. If we can get it in our hearts to pray until God speaks, it will change *everything*.

Eli finally saw the burden this woman carried and spoke a promise over her. This was her word. He told her to go in peace and that God would fulfill her request. Hannah got up from her place of desperate prayer, wiped the tears from her face, put on a smile, and walked out with her head held high. Scripture states that her countenance, or her facial expressions, had completely changed; she was no longer sad. She received a Word from the Lord. She had no doubt in her mind that her God would come through. The man of God had spoken, and she was eager to receive it. The only thing left to do at this moment was to *stand* on that promise and *wait* on the Lord to bring it to pass.

Waiting. What a hard thing to do, or so it seems. But by definition, according to the 1828 Webster's Dictionary, waiting simply means "staying in expectation". What God has spoken will surely come to pass (Ezekiel 12:25). There isn't much we can trust in our present world, but we can trust in Him.

The very next scripture states "they rose up in the morning early and worshiped before the Lord" (1 Samuel 1:19). After they returned home from church, Hannah and her husband were intimate. Just like that, after all this time of heartache and tiresome waiting, Hannah conceived a son.

God remembered her request.

He showed His faithfulness to Hannah, and she was ready to keep her vow to Him. She named her son Samuel, which literally means "heard of God" or "God has heard." Samuel was to be a consecrated man mightily used by the Lord. Like Samson's, Hannah's vow that no razor would touch the hair of his head was a portion of the Nazarite vow, a vow of ultimate consecration and of diligently separating oneself from anything unclean or common to remain pure and holy before a Holy God. He would mature to be an incredible prophet of God. And guess what? He was born from a woman who endured some seemingly impossible seasons and ultimately trusted in her God to see her through. What a beautiful testimony.

"Sing, O heavens; and be joyful, O earth; and break forth into singing, O mountains: for the LORD hath comforted his people, and will have mercy upon his afflicted."

Isaiah 49:13

11

The God Who Remembers

I have always loved the name Samuel. Until recently I was certain I would name my future son Samuel. When someone asks what we think our promised baby will be or what gender we want when we finally conceive, my husband and I have always been very confident our first child would be a son. Every barren womb of the Bible is opened with a son; it just seems to me like that is God's plan. I have heard stories of women struggling with infertility and having girls, but we both just feel so confident that our miracle would be a son. Most of the dreams that I have had which have included a child who I felt was obviously my own was often a blond-haired little boy. And he was perfect.

Like Hannah, I've had periods in this journey with infertility where I had cried out to the Lord in desperation. I've also vowed that I would surrender my own son to His will and for His purpose if He would grant me the desires of my heart. I promised to train him in the way that he should walk, teaching him the Word of God and how to live a godly life. I asked God for strength and wisdom to be the mother that He created me to be, and the mother I would need to be in order to successfully raise up this child to be obedient to His Word. Like Manoah, I wanted to know what I should or shouldn't do with the child God would give me. I frequently prayed, "God if you give him to me, I will give him to you!"

Before I found out I was pregnant for the very first time in March 2023, I was at Costco picking up pizzas for a small group my husband and I led at our church. There was a father with two young boys, potentially between ages two and four running around behind me. The dad lovingly called out, "Judah, Judah," and my heart melted at the sound of that name. I immediately thought, "oh no! Why do I love that name so much?" Would this name take the place of Samuel, a name I had been so adamant on choosing for when we became pregnant? I seriously was very worried about that!

That night at life group, a friend that we affectionately call "Mama Pat" had just come back from vacation. In the past, she frequently looked at me and said, "You're pregnant." Spiritually, she sees it. If anyone else would say that to me, I'd probably kindly ask them to never do that again, but I know her heart, so I allowed it to continue. In this particular case, she was right. We just didn't know it yet. Those comments can be so hurtful to someone who wants to be and has never ever been. There have been times I have had to discreetly tell someone those comments were extremely hurtful although I know they did not intend them to be, and I'd ensure them that I would tell them as soon as I could when I was.

At this life group, we somehow started speaking as a group on what our future child would be. So, I called out to Joey and said, "What is our baby going to be?" Without hesitation, he responded, "a boy opens the womb." I'm almost certain others in the group thought we were pregnant right then. I told Mama Pat about what happened at Costco with the name "Judah" that I had spoken of in a previous chapter of this book.

She looked at me with the biggest smile on her face and said, "Judah means praise."

God has a thing about names. He changed Abram's name to Abraham., Sarai to Sarah, Jacob to Israel. Even God Himself has a changed name. In the Old Testament, the children of Israel knew Him as Yahweh (or Jehovah), the I Am. New Testament believers know Him as Jesus, God with us (John 1:1, 14, Matthew 1:21.23). The name Jesus literally means "Jehovah is the Savior" or "Jehovah saves." He's the same God (Deuteronomy 6:4, Isaiah 9:6, Colossians 2:9), but His relationship with His people changed, and that warranted a new name.

Samuel was a name from a different season for me, a season that was long and dry. But Judah was a rekindled promise, a new covenant. My journey changed course, and God was about to show me that I could praise Him even in my hurting and my pain.

Two days later, I found out I was pregnant for the first time in our church bathroom. I'd always wanted to find out there. I often daydreamed of what that day might be like when I would see two lines for the very first time on a pregnancy test. He brought that dream to pass. He sees me! And the timing of this was not a coincidence. He is a God of details and cares for the things that we care for. Every romantic or sentimental piece of our being is in His likeness. We are made in His image. If we care about these small little things, how much more does He care about them? What a beautiful God we serve! His heart is like no other.

God, you amaze me and astound me with who You are! You truly are an *awe*-some God!

When the Bible says God remembered Hannah, it brings such joy and warmth to my heart. We do not serve a God who has short term memory loss. He does not need us to remind Him over and over of what we need or what He said. He knows. He remembers. Jeremiah 29:11-13 tells us that God thinks of us, each and every one of us. Think of someone you love beyond measure in this life. How often does that person cross your mind? You and I cross the mind of God. And when He thinks of us, He thinks of all the things we need, desire, and of ways to make Himself known to us.

My husband will randomly call me throughout the day if he has not heard from me. He knows I have a busy job and am in meetings quite frequently which means I can't answer, but without fail each day he calls. He wouldn't call if I didn't cross his mind. Most of the time he doesn't want or need anything other than to know what I'm doing. He ,too, is made in the image of God! These characteristics were inherited from God Himself. Likewise, if my day is busy and I've gone a period of time without calling upon or checking in with the Lord, He will think of me and interact with me in a way that gets my attention. He calls me. He remembers me. In the darkest moments of my life, I'm thankful I serve a God who is thinking of me and remembers my pain.

Sometime after Hannah received her promise, it was time for the yearly sacrifice. This meant her family would travel to the house of God and it wasn't just down the street. Hannah could have taken the journey with her husband, but instead she chose to stay back until Samuel was weaned. "Then," she said, "I will bring him that he may appear before the Lord, and there abide forever" (1 Samuel 1:22). Her husband's response causes me to think that it wouldn't have been uncommon for a woman with an infant to go. He simply said, "Do what seemeth thee good" (1 Samuel 1:23). She could choose to go or choose to stay. It was completely up to her.

I don't know if what I'm about to say is accurate. The Bible doesn't give us the details of what was going on in her heart, but from my perspective this makes complete sense. Hear me out. Hannah vowed that she would give Samuel to the Lord for the rest of his life. Could it have been that she did not want to go to the house of God and return home with the son she promised to Him? Did she feel that it might appear like she wasn't keeping her end of the deal? He wasn't weaned yet and it would be difficult for him to care for himself. Her plan to follow through on her promise to the Lord was to go there and leave him in the presence of God to grow up in the house of God. So, she refrained from going to the temple until she could safely leave him.

In my personal life, I have made some commitments that would prove to be significant sacrifices. I even felt led by God to make those commitments, and sometimes with such an urgency. But when I put those commitments into practice, I couldn't ignore the overwhelming feeling that the timing wasn't quite right. If I chose to act upon them anyway (typically out of fear or desperation), I inevitably failed and eventually (regrettably) became desensitized to the burden I once felt to bring those sacrifices forth. This made it extremely difficult to follow through when the right time finally came. Fasting for an extended period of time is just one example.

    Hannah finally had her son. The prayer she prayed in deep sorrow was now in her arms. She knew giving him up would not be easy, but God kept His promise and now she had to keep hers. Some references indicate that weaning could have been completed anytime between the ages of three and nine years old. She had time to prepare herself to act on her promise. She undoubtedly cherished the time she spent with him, knowing that soon her time with him would be limited to yearly trips to the temple to worship and sacrifice to the Lord.

    When the time finally came, Hannah confidently entered the house of God. She had a sacrifice that was unlike any other, and such a price it was! She presented Samuel to Eli the priest and said, "O my lord, I am the woman that stood by thee here, praying unto the LORD" (1 Samuel 1:26). "Eli, do you remember when I was in such desperation that I ran to the house of God and poured my soul out unto the Lord? Remember that I was so distraught at the weight of my grief that you thought I was drunken? Do you remember what you said to me, that God would grant the desires of my heart?" I can imagine Hannah holding the child to get Eli's attention. "For this child I prayed: and the LORD hath given me my petition which I asked of him" (1 Samuel 1:27). "Eli, this is my son. Here he is before you. This is the child that I prayed for, and God was faithful to provide what I asked of Him."

    Hannah explained that she brought Samuel to the house of the Lord to give Him to the Lord as long as he lives. Her greatest joy was to know that her child would be a servant of the most high God: the God that sees and hears, the God that remembers, the merciful and faithful God that keeps His promises. Hannah prayed a beautiful prayer before leaving Samuel to the service of the Lord. She visited every year at the time of the yearly sacrifice and brought with her a little coat she made for him that would serve as a token of her motherly love.

God blessed her faithfulness to His kingdom by opening her womb to conceive five additional children. You cannot outgive God, no matter the price! What a wonderful God we serve! She was content with what she had, yet God blessed her exceeding abundantly above what her heart could think or imagine.

Each of us has a purpose, and if our steps are truly being led by the prompting of the Lord, then we can rest assured trusting that He has a plan for the circumstances we find ourselves in. He sees the end of sorrow, grief, and pain. This journey is incredibly hard, and not many people quite understand what it is like to endure a season with a barren womb. But God sees you. He hears you. And He will remember you.

" He will fulfill the desire of them that fear him: he also will hear their cry, and will save them"

Psalm 145:19

12

It Shall Be Well

There's something about an old dusty hymnal and the treasures inside that hits a special place within my heart. In my opinion, the worse shape it's in, the better. I can imagine the saints of God from generations before us singing the songs inside that have never lost their power. The truth is, the songs themselves only have power because they tell of One who has *all* power. They talk of trials of life and storms we must weather while clinging to an old, rugged cross on a hill far away, and the wonder working power of the blood of the Lamb that came to remit our sin and shame. Amidst whatever this natural life can bring our way, we have a blessed assurance that He is in control. He is the great Shepherd, and He is still on the throne.

There's an old song that you may know. It goes a little like this:

"When peace like a river attendeth my way
When sorrows like sea billows roll
Whatever my lot, Thou has taught me to say
It is well, it is well with my soul
(Horatio Gates Spafford & Philip Paul Bliss, 1873)

This scriptural phrase, "It is well," is commonly used throughout Christianity and even in the secular world. It's posted on stickers and magnets, car windows, coffee cups, clothing, and more. But many years ago, about 900 B.C., there was a great woman in the land of Shunem. For her, it wasn't just a nice catch phrase. This statement testified of a peace she found and would not forsake no matter what circumstances she faced. A peace so constant the winds that blow in some of the fiercest storms of life could not shake it. I find it interesting that the name of this city means "quietly." There was a stillness, a peaceful calm, a quiet resolve about this great woman.

Like Manoah's wife, we will never know her name. These two ladies were ordinary women who the world did not know on a deeper level or perhaps were never more than acquaintances. They probably weren't very popular in their culture or in elevated statuses among their social circles, and were likely known by their humility and generosity instead of their name. Yet God saw fit for them to be included in His Word. More importantly, He chose them to be an example for women to follow when the storms of this life rage around us. I have found great encouragement as I've journeyed through the pages of scripture that contain their stories.

If you haven't read about her, you can probably guess that this woman of Shunem had a great need. Her husband was old, and she had no child (2 Kings 4:14). Unlike many of the other women, scripture does not specifically say she was barren. However, when studying this woman, I've come across many articles from Jewish sources that list her among the barren women of the Bible.

I've participated in community forums for women trying to conceive and it is equally as heart wrenching for women who are in situations in which their spouses were diagnosed with infertility. There are more other occasions when the reason for the lack of conception is considered "unidentified," even after both parties are thoroughly tested. This historical account in scripture simply states that her husband was old, and she was childless. Without any additional information, we will assume she was also barren. Regardless of the state of her womb, conception did not occur, and it undoubtedly affected her.

Thankfully, there was a man of God in her life who often journeyed through her city. Each time he passed through, she would constrain him to come in to eat bread (2 Kings 4:8). The word "constrain" in this verse means to fasten upon, to seize, bind, or conquer. In other words, this woman would not take no for an answer! As he continued to pass through the neighborhood, she said to her husband, "this man is a holy man of God who passes by here frequently and we need to give him a space to turn into." It's obvious that she cared about his well-being and wanted to give him a place to rest, but I wonder if it may be that she also wanted him to linger? There's something about men and women of God who live for God diligently, those who are consecrated and have completely separated themselves from the values of this world. These men and women are all in.

My husband and I were at a camp meeting in Sterling, Alaska, in June 2023. He was ordained and it was such a special atmosphere. We were surrounded by men and women of God who had sacrificed it all for the sake of the Kingdom, and God had used them mightily in ministry. As the days passed, a bittersweet feeling arose in my heart. I knew the time would come and go, and I just wanted to spend as much time with them as I could while I was still in their presence. I tried to get up early and often stayed up late. I'd try to get to the tabernacle early, and in between services, I would check out the cafeteria where I thought some of these men and women might be having fellowship. I wanted to hear their stories and glean from their wisdom. I remember almost feeling a little sad the day that we left. I told my husband, "This is what Heaven is going to be like: like-minded people of faith speaking of the goodness of God and praising Him for all that He has done without being hindered by the hustle and bustle of this busy world full of distractions." It was so encouraging. I can imagine it would have been similarly or even more so encouraging for her.

Feeling the burden to care for this man of God who was due to pass by any day now, the place she prepared for him was stocked beyond the essentials. A bed to rest upon would have been sufficient, but she insisted on including a table, a stool, and a candlestick. She was presenting him with an opportunity to stay a while. Sure enough, Elisha and his servant turned into the little chamber she had set up. In return for her generosity and kindness, he wanted to bless her. Her response to his request indicated that all she had was sufficient for her. She was peacefully content with her position in life and wanted nothing more than to care for the man of God in honor of the One he served.

I love the way Matthew Henry's commentary speaks to this situation:

"The Lord sees the secret wish which is suppressed in obedience to His will, and He will hear the prayers of His servants on behalf of their benefactors, by sending unasked-for and unexpected mercies."

He honors a humble, obedient, and sacrificial heart. Solomon could have had whatever he asked God for, but all he requested was wisdom so that he could go about his days and respond to life's demands in a manner that would bring glory to the King of Kings. Because of his noble request, God gave him that and more! He blessed Solomon beyond measure (2 Chronicles 1:7-12). Likewise, God saw the heart of this Shunamite woman who worried about the well-being of this godly man, and wanted to make sure anything he could possibly need was presented to him during his stay. Elisha saw that she took a great amount of thought in the project at hand, and he wanted her to be fruitful for her labor. At her humble response, Elisha asked his servant, "What can we do for this great woman?" His servant simply stated, "she has no child." Elisha knew the significant impact this likely had on her and said, "About this season, according to the time of life, thou shalt embrace a son" (2 Kings 4:16a).

Embrace. Something she likely dreamt of and longed for. I bet she couldn't imagine what it might feel like to embrace a son that she conceived, carried, and birthed into this world, a son she longed for with all of her heart for an unknown period of time.

She replied, "Nay, my lord, thou man of God, do not lie unto thine handmaid" (2 Kings 4:16b). In other words, "Elisha, you are a man of God. I trust and have confidence in your walk with Him, but please don't make this promise to me. You don't know what I've been through or how painful this journey has been. My heart is content. I've dealt with my feelings and I'm at peace with never being a mother. Please don't stir up those feelings once again within my heart. I can't bear to relive the devastation I know I will feel if this doesn't come to pass like you say it will."

Oh, how I can relate!

I don't know how many times women and even men of God who upon hearing that my husband and I were unable to have children would say, "God is able." While I know that is true and according to His Word, it's sometimes accompanied with an awkwardness on both parts as if no one else knows what to say next. Sometimes, there's a saint of God who has a tremendous measure of faith based on what God has answered in their own lives and the testimonies He has allowed them to witness, and they have spoken over me that God will be true to His promise in giving me the desires of my heart, proclaiming that I shall conceive in His timing. I have even had some go as far as purchasing gifts for my future son. In specific times of life when I searched for an answer, prayed for Him to speak, and diligently inclined my ear to hear His voice, those comments and gestures were comforting. They ignited hope and faith within me. I considered them a confirmation and an answered prayer, a reminder that God was indeed working on my behalf. But the majority of the time those comments were unsolicited and unwanted, stinging like daggers piercing the innermost portions of my heart, the deepest places that I tried to hide and protect with all that I had.

"Please don't give me false hope," she likely thought.

But once again, God completely changed the course of this woman's life. He brought beauty out of ashes, and she conceived a son at precisely the season Elisha told her she would. God is always on time! She thought it was too late, and God said, "this is just the time I was waiting for!"

And they lived happily ever after. . .

Well, not quite.

One day while out with his father, her son became very ill. His father sent him to his mother who held him – literally *embraced* him – upon her knees until he took his last breath around the middle of the day. At the sight of what seemed to be like a dead promise, she picked up his lifeless body, walked into the space she had prepared for the man of God, laid him upon the bed, and shut the door (2 Kings 4:21). She called her husband who knew the child had been ill and told him she would need to go to the man of God. Her husband questioned why she would need to go to the prophet at this time, as it was not the typical time to go to him for instruction. She simply said, "It *shall* be well." Actually, the phrase listed here was a single word in the ancient Hebrew text and that word was "shalom" which is simply "peace."

"There was no need to worry," she declared. She received a promise, and she was not going to allow her promise to die.

A verse in scripture we all know well is Philippians 4:7 which states "The peace of God, which passeth all understanding, shall keep your hearts and minds through Christ Jesus." This peace is what this brave woman of God possessed that stood guard to protect her thoughts from running rampant with negativity and fear or influencing her perception of what was happening before her eyes. By the standards of the world, it was over. Her child was dead. There's no coming back from that. Death is final. She likely had not seen someone raised from the dead. If she allowed it, her experiences would agree with the world's perception, which likely would have instilled hopelessness and sorrow into her heart. So where does this peace come from? We could agree that it comes from God, but how can one person experience peace in the loss of a child and another the absolute absence of peace? The answer is one verse prior. "Be careful for nothing; but in every thing by prayer and supplication with thanksgiving let your requests be made known unto God" (Philippians 4:6). Don't be anxious or burdened by worry. Instead, with a thankful heart, trust that He is in control and bring every request to Him. Only then can His peace that exceeds far beyond all human logic and reasoning encompass your heart and keep your heart and mind stayed on Him. We must *choose* to cast down every fearful thought that attempts to exalt itself above our knowledge of God (2 Corinthians 10:5), knowing He is for us and not against us, and will not withhold any good thing from those that walk uprightly (Psalm 84:11).

In the darkest hour, she chose to not give in to worry or anxiety. Instead, even in what seemed to be the death of her promised son, she chose peace. This doesn't mean that she didn't feel the effects of what happened or that this loss wasn't incredibly difficult to bear. In 2 Kings 4:27, Elisha told his servant that her soul was "vexed within her." The word "soul" in scripture often refers to the mind or heart. She was absolutely heartbroken. There was a deep grief and bitterness in her soul. But her response to this tragedy shows us that she had a relationship with the one true God, the same God that parted the Red Sea and provided manna in the wilderness for several decades, sustaining His people. The same God that said He would never leave or forsake those who walked according to His statutes.

She ran to the man of God and challenged him at his word. "Did I desire a son of my lord? Did I not say, do not deceive me?" (2 Kings 4:28). She accepted her course in life and surrendered that desire for motherhood long ago, and yet it was this man of God's will that she conceived a son. She did all that she could do by embracing her son until his dying breath. Now it was time to allow him to do what only he could do by the power of the One he served.

If God has spoken a promise over you, don't be afraid to challenge Him at His Word. He can take it! Especially if the word came from the mouth of man. He admonishes in His Word to "try the spirit whether they are of God" (1 John 4:1). All throughout scripture, mighty men and women of God remind Him of what He had spoken or of His nature.

Abraham challenged God when He tried to overthrow Sodom and

Gomorrah. "God, will you really destroy the righteous with the wicked? This doesn't seem like you!" (Genesis 18:23). The psalmist questions what seems to be God's anger toward His people in Psalm 85: 5-6: "Will you be angry with us forever? Will you not revive us again?" These are just a few examples of men and women of God essentially saying, "Lord, You are good, just, merciful, and faithful." They knew Him well enough to know what to expect of Him. "I will hear what God the LORD will speak: for He will speak peace unto His people " (Psalm 85:8).

When it was apparent that I was miscarrying my first pregnancy, I could imagine how this woman of God must have felt. I had surrendered my desire for motherhood to Him and submitted to His will, regardless of what that might look like for my future. As I mentioned previously, when I found out I was expecting, I felt the pregnancy was invincible. It was the hand of God and there was no doubt about that! I will share the full details of my pregnancy and all that transpired later in this book, but when I started having some complications shortly after finding out I was pregnant, I had a deep sense of anxiety and worry. It was a constant battle to choose peace instead of giving in to the intense thoughts of worry and dread. I admit that I could have allowed bitterness to rise up within me. I prayed fervently and cried out to God declaring, "God, you would not give me this and then take it from me. I _know_ you!" Ultimately, I had to surrender even that pregnancy to Him and trust in His will for my life and for the life that struggled to grow within me. When I received the news, that the pregnancy hormone levels in my blood had dropped, indicating that I was miscarrying, I went to my private place of prayer in my home and laid this pregnancy on the altar. I cried out to God and reminded Him that this was His hand that caused this pregnancy. I reminded Him of the promises He spoke to me through His Word, the confirmation after confirmation He had shown me leading up to my positive test, and I had to _choose_ peace despite the agonizing reality that was hitting me like a ton of bricks: my promise was dying and there's nothing I could do. I was not in control.

Truthfully, there _was_ something I could do, and it was all I could do, all I was really required to do. Here's the key in surviving what seems to be the death of a promise: *let go* and surrender control to the only One trustworthy enough to use whatever the circumstances may be and turn it for your good. The latter end will be even better than the former. I promise. Actually, God promises (Haggai 2:9, Job 8:7). And He can be held to His Word.

    This woman was able to mother her child. Later in the child's life, God was able to use her story as a testimony to show others what a faithful God she served. As for me, the truth is despite what it looked like and what the world wanted me to believe, my promise was not dead. I realized God was calling me into a deeper level of consecration, spiritual intimacy, and trust in Him. That pregnancy birthed a stronger commitment and a peace that is unmeasurable. Now, only because of Him allowing me to experience this season of tragic loss, there is no doubt in my mind that God can do this! In fact, there's no doubt in my mind that God can do anything! He continues to prove Himself faithful not only to others but to me, even in circumstances that seem impossible and when all hope feels lost. And although now He doesn't have to, He continues to speak His promise to me. He has shown me through my own experiences that He is a promise keeper.

"The LORD of hosts hath sworn, saying, Surely as I have thought, so shall it come to pass; and as I have purposed, so shall it stand."

Isaiah 14:24

13

A New Day is Dawning

When God led the children of Israel under Joshua's command to the city of Jericho, Joshua was already aware that it was going to be a fenced city. He had sent two men to spy out the land, yet the obstacle in their way of victory did not automatically cause their hearts to resound defeat. Whatever is in our way should not intimidate us either. The children of Israel didn't need heavy artillery to cause those walls to fall. They faced a spiritual battle far greater than the physical battle their eyes could see. Carnal weapons were powerless against their true opponent.

Throughout the entire Bible, God uses types and shadows to teach us deeper spiritual concepts using things we can see and our finite minds can understand to help us comprehend the deeper things of the spiritual realm. These physical illustrations show us just how mighty He is, empowering us to avoid the snares the enemy lays before us to attempt to derail God's plan.

In the case for Jericho, it may seem a little silly that God chose trumpets as the weapons of war. He spoke to Joshua "I have given unto thine hand Jericho, and ye shall compass the city, all ye men of war, and go around about the city once. Thus, shalt thou do six days. And seven priests shall bear before the ark seven trumpets of rams horns: and it shall come to pass, that when they make a long blast with the ram's horn, and when ye hear the sound of the trumpet, all the people shall shout with a great shout; and the wall of the city shall fall down flat" (Joshua 6:2-5). Joshua led the children of Israel around the city of Jericho once each day for six days and the only sound made was of the priests bearing the trumpets. The people were instructed to not make a sound until they heard the trumpet on the seventh day after marching around the city seven times.

As they made their way around the city each day, the Ark of the Covenant of God followed them. The Ark of the Covenant was a testimony of all that God had done as well as a reminder of what He promised to do, and it was continuously with them as they walked along the walls of this city. It was not just a reminder for the children of Israel, but for everyone they would come against. It showed that the Israelites were not fighting their own battles, but their God was fighting for them, and the victory was already won.

While God dealt with each of them and led them to trust in Him, He also dealt with their enemies. The people of Jericho knew the Israelites were coming for their city, and they had heard of the power of their God. In fact, when Joshua scouted out the city, Rahab told him that she knew the Lord had given them the land and that all the inhabitants of the city were fearful because they had heard all that the Lord had done. "As soon as we had heard these things, our hearts did melt, and neither did there remain any more courage in any man, because of you: for the Lord your God, He is God in heaven above and in earth beneath" (Joshua 2:11).

On the seventh day when that trumpet blew and the Israelites lifted up their voice in a shout, the walls of Jericho fell. Similarly, despite how bleak and grim our circumstances may seem, when we lift up a shout of praise to our most high God, possessor of heaven and earth, our praise bears witness of who He is, what He has done. Our faith grows as we witness what He is capable of doing.

It's easy to lift up a shout of praise after witnessing a victory in a battle we have faced, but as born-again believers who rest in confidence of our mighty God, we must be diligent to employ the discipline of praise even before our eyes have seen the fruits of a victorious battle, knowing that God knows the plans He has for us and already sees the end. We must learn to leave the details to Him and trust He is fighting for us!

In previous chapters, I shared bits and pieces of my own struggle with infertility and loss. At a pivotal point in my walk with God, He used a Jericho type situation to teach me the true meaning and power of praise. Our church commits to prayer and fasting every January for the entire month. Our associate pastor puts out a calendar and we all make a discreet mark on the days we commit to prayer and fasting. At the end of the month, we bind together in unity for a corporate three-day fast. In January 2023, I committed to pray and fast one 24-hour period during a weekday and a 48-hour fast each weekend throughout the month. The month would end in a corporate 3-day fast alongside our church congregation. I also committed to pray every day for 20 mins in the morning, and again in the evening, not including my typical prayers throughout the day or my Bible reading time. I enjoyed and looked forward to my time in the Lord.

The World Network of Prayer (WNOP) also had a time of prayer and fasting for the month of January. The theme this year was "Open." Along with the prayer points they had sent out; I began to pray for an open womb. One of the scriptures of focused prayer was Matthew 21:22 "And all things, whatsoever ye shall ask in prayer, believing, ye shall receive ". I felt my faith rising and memorized this verse, reciting it almost every day.

On my prayer wall in my prayer room is a cork board with special memorials, reminders for me to continue to praise God and pray for these situations. Hanging on that prayer board was a small piece of paper with the evidence of the miracle God performed for me highlighting the results of my hormones and other lab levels that miraculously returned to normal levels after being anointed and prayed for at our church. I've given an account of this in an earlier chapter. I noticed on that paper the luteinizing hormone

(LH) level, the hormone responsible for ovulation, was 6.66. While in the normal range, those numbers that signified the result struck me spiritually. It felt like a spiritual attack from the enemy on my fertility. Remember that definition of barrenness? It literally means to root up or destroy completely the reproductive organs. I rebuked that attack in the name of Jesus Christ with authority and by the power that He gave me according to His Word. I commanded every cell in my body that was in rebellion to the design and function God had created them for in the very beginning to be obedient to the Lord. I began to claim God's promises over my life.

At some point in my time of prayer and fasting that month, I felt God told me the things He had spoken to me or prepared me for in 2022, He would bring to pass in 2023. He also showed me that He would "do a new thing." He gave me Isaiah 43:18-19: "Remember ye not the *former* things, neither consider the things of old. Behold, I will do a *new* thing; _now_ shall it spring forth; shall ye not know it? I will even make a way in the wilderness, and rivers in the desert." I had no idea what this meant, but there was such an urgency in the "now shall it spring forth; shall ye not know it?" and I wanted to be ready to see God's hand moving on my behalf. I wanted my spiritual eyes opened and focused on Him so that I would not be distracted and miss the blessings He had in store for me.

Each day, God spoke to me in subtle ways regarding this promise. I received daily confirmations that He was hearing me. After over fourteen years of contemplating birth plans, I decided I would love to have a stress-free, all-natural home birth. One day as my mind was astray with thoughts of what this day may look like for me, a fearful thought entered my mind. I feared that we lived too far out of town, too far away from an ambulance if something were to go wrong during the delivery.

It was later that evening or the evening after that I was coming home from some errands on the other side of town and decided to take a different route. I was caught up in my thoughts and this area of my community was unfamiliar to me. I thought I missed my turn, so I began to focus and diligently pay close attention to my surroundings. A short few moments later, I passed the Emergency Medical Services (EMS) station where the fire trucks and ambulances were parked. I felt excitement rise within me and set my odometer. It was only three miles from my house.

I felt like this was an answered prayer and that God was telling me He has everything under control. It was also a confirmation that God does have a plan for me to conceive and birth a child. This was no coincidence. He cared about what I cared about, and I could trust Him.

During this time of prayer and fasting, I felt a burden to pray for my husband and pleaded with God to allow Joey to be a dad. I wanted him to be awarded the opportunity to prove himself a better father than his father. I prayed the generational curses that plagued his family and upbringing would stop with him and he would not follow in his father's footsteps. I praised God for what He had brought Joey from, and I fervently prayed for God to redeem that part of his life.

Joey and his sisters had no positive memories of his father who had left when he was a young child. It wasn't until Joey was in his 30s and began to live for Jesus that he could speak with his father and voice his forgiveness. Unfortunately, the only contact he had with him was through a few instant messages and phone calls in the hospital before he passed away. I remember what I felt in that moment of prayer. It was such a sweet prayer unto the Lord, and I wept hard under the power of that burden for my husband.

This was a beautiful time of hearing clearly the voice of the Lord. It encouraged me and showed me that the journey I had been on so far was not in vain. This was not an empty promise. I could praise Him for all He had done. There would be a day coming when this darkness I felt I was wandering through would end.

The dawn was coming . . .

And I could see it . . .

"We have also a more sure word of prophecy; whereunto ye do well that ye take heed, as unto a light that shineth in a dark place, until the day dawn, and the day star arise in your hearts"

2 Peter 1:19

14

I Will Do a New Thing

Only ten days after my thirty-one days of devoted special consecration ended, I started noticing I was more fatigued than normal. I also started having some changes in my body which indicated that things were changing in my reproductive cycle as well as some mild cramps. I decided to track my symptoms on a fertility app. A few days after these symptoms started, I took a home pregnancy test which was negative. My heart soared, though, when the app showed the symptoms, I charted indicated a fertile period. I don't believe I have ever seen this before! I continued to pray and believe in God for a miracle.

Our district's Ministers and Wives Retreat was scheduled for the end of the month. I thought about how wonderful it would be to find out there among all the people who witnessed the prayer Bro. Cornwell prayed over us at camp in 2019. I spoke of this in an earlier chapter as well. I thought, "what a testimony! What a time of rejoicing that will be!" I was excited to see what God was going to do. It was a joyful time of waiting on the Lord, expecting to be expecting.

At work one day not long after this, one of my newer employees told me she thought I was pregnant due to my extreme fatigue. We shared an office, and she knew part of my struggle with infertility. She didn't want to say anything to me that may hurt my feelings. On another occasion. I used some lotion from an employee that smelled like peppermint patties. I remember leaving work that day and craving them so badly that I went to a nearby health food store. I was trying diligently to avoid sugar as much as possible and I thought surely, they'd have something similar that was healthier. I was wrong. I purchased a chocolate covered coconut bar as it was the closest thing to a peppermint patty that I could find and was disappointed because it just wasn't the same.

February 21, the Tuesday right before Ministers and Wives retreat, I took another pregnancy test, and it was also negative. The retreat was in Anchorage which is about 350 miles from where we lived at the time and took about seven hours on average to drive there. We stopped at a few convenience stores along the way, and I thought to myself, "If they have peppermint patties, I'm getting some." I just couldn't take it any longer and needed to satisfy the craving. Sure enough, they did, and they were amazing! I also bought a large bottle of cucumber lime flavored water, and it had never tasted quite as good as it did on that day. I noticed down the road that I had finished the entire bottle in a relatively short amount of time. I don't typically feel thirsty, and when I drink something, it is usually not water. When I do drink water, it's carbonated, not flat. I was quite astonished that I was so thirsty all of a sudden and drank the entire bottle with very little effort in a short amount of time. I kept all these things in my heart and kept clinging to the promise that God gave me.

I was so exhausted the entire way and napped a good bit of the ride. Usually, it's a pretty impossible feat for me to sleep in a car, even if driving overnight. And for this trip, we drove in the middle of the day. Much to my surprise, I was thrilled when we arrived, and I found that the church hosting the retreat had a huge candy jar full of mini peppermint patties! Sis. Heather Blackshear, if you ever read this, thank you for being led by the Lord. I am convinced those peppermint patties were just for me!

I really believe it!

God is such a romantic and details matter to Him!

Bro. Tim Gaddy was one of our speakers for that event. During one of his messages, he mentioned that he always takes a nap. We joked during the afternoon breaks, that we had to take naps, too, because he preached it. I mean, we *had* to be obedient to the man of God in our lives, right? It gave us an excuse to take naps between sessions, which those of us who were traveling together all took advantage of. I actually napped every day. This was completely out of the ordinary for me. I usually can't force my mind to relax enough during the day to nap. If my husband wants to take a nap, I will often lay down with him in an attempt to rest, but I usually end up laying there awake reading or looking up random useless facts on my phone, trying my hardest not to make noise or disturb him. This particular week, I was exhausted. And I actually slept!

I tested again two days later, and again it was negative. I had such an expectation for a positive test. I was waiting for it.

At one of the night sessions, I asked two ladies who knew my story to pray with me. I told them I felt pregnant but was getting negative tests. During one of the sessions, one of the ministers in our district came up to me and my husband and told me he never forgot about the prayer Bro. Cornwell prayed over us at that camp meeting. He laid his hand on me and prayed again. It was more an act of faith in receiving those things that were spoken over us than a prayer, but I kept it in my heart. I knew God was doing something. I didn't mention to him that I thought I was currently pregnant.

That Saturday morning, two days after the previous test, I tested again. It was negative. I told myself if it was still negative on Monday, I'd go to get a blood test. When that day came, the test was negative, as well as the following day. My cramping, fatigue, and some of the other symptoms I had experienced were almost gone. Because of this, I decided not to get the blood test and to go on with life just as I had every other time in the past fourteen years that I had convinced myself this might actually be it!

The following weekend was extremely difficult and emotional, as one may imagine it to be following my drastic plummet back down to planet earth. Looking back now, though, I can see that it was different, more extreme and even irrational. I have friends who planted a church in a nearby town, and that Friday night my husband preached at their church as the pastor and his wife were on vacation.

Sis. Kristin, the assistant pastor's wife and a good friend of mine, sat in my car with me in her driveway until about 1 a.m. I told her I was feeling down and offloaded with a lot of my emotions. I was felt extremely low emotionally and spiritually and was overwhelmed with all of the responsibilities we had committed to at work and at church, honestly with life in general. I really wanted to slow down and rest more. The demands of constantly having to be somewhere or do something were affecting me on a level I wasn't prepared for. It was almost debilitating.

I spoke to my pastor a few months prior about pulling out of some things. I felt guilty for even thinking about it, and ended up not pulling out of much despite his admonition to ensure I wasn't overcommitted and headed for burnout. This particular night I decided that it really was time. The following day, I pulled out of all the church work I was involved in except for our small group ministry and our church bookstore.

I thought it was stress affecting my energy levels and my ability to think straight. I was extremely scatter-brained, and I locked myself out of the house one day. Everything made me more emotional than it should have. I was completely irrational in many ways. It was freezing outside, and in Alaska that doesn't mean 32 degrees above zero. It gets cold here. I'm not sure what the temperature was, but it was not safe to be outside without proper cold gear for a period of time. I was wearing dress boots and did not have my snow skirt on. Thankfully, my car was unlocked and provided some shelter from the elements, until a dear friend of mine that lived about 15 minutes away was able to come rescue me. I felt like I was losing my mind. All I wanted to do was nap and the housework was getting majorly behind. I felt guilty and couldn't understand why I suddenly became so lazy. On the other hand, I enjoyed my period of rest. I needed it, mentally and physically.

My cravings ramped up and although I was supposed to be avoiding flour, I craved pizza. Since I was on this emotional rollercoaster and had reached the upper limits of my self-control, I decided to cave and order gluten free pizza. The following day, that same dear friend and her family wanted to go out to dinner after church, and of course the restaurant we chose had gluten free pizza also. The next day, Monday, I realized that pizza was also the theme for dinner at our small group that week. I knew my husband wouldn't be happy as he was probably growing very bored with it by now, but I was thrilled!

One night as I laid awake unable to sleep, I watched birth vlogs of home births with twins. I've always had this feeling that we would one day mother twins. I have daydreamed of this since childhood. Joey's granddad was a twin, and although what I've researched states the contrary, I've always heard that twins run in families and usually fall on the boy's side. Sure enough, there was an account of a successful home birth for twins at full term. God was relieving any fear or concern that I had, even without me asking Him to. He was showing me that He sees me. He has this situation under control. It was a constant daily reminder that my steps are ordered, and I have nothing to fear. He has this in His hands. I can trust Him.

That Thursday night, I couldn't sleep, and I became more and more frustrated with my symptoms, the instances of what seemed to be confirmations from the Lord, and these negative pregnancy tests. I looked up an OBGYN and decided to make an appointment. I started having sore breasts the day before and they were becoming very uncomfortable. This soreness was completely different than some of the earlier sensitivities and soreness I had a few weeks before that faded. I wanted a blood test or an ultrasound to tell me what was happening in my body. I was also having some cramping, and the cramping was more severe than before. It wasn't painful, but I felt a heaviness in my uterus that was bizarre. These symptoms were different than I'd ever felt before. In fact, I felt different altogether. The next morning, Friday March 10, I called an OB. I was so preoccupied by my symptoms that I couldn't concentrate at work. The OB that I had found the night before during my period of insomnia couldn't get me in until the beginning of April. I didn't want to wait that long. I *couldn't* wait that long. I needed an answer right then.

I looked into the wait times at an urgent care in our hospital system for which I work. It was an hour and half. I really didn't want to miss work as I had some things to do that day that needed to be done before the weekend, and I needed to run to Walmart to grab a few things for Men's Breakfast at our church the next day. If I went to urgent care, I'd be late for church and would have to go to Walmart afterwards. I was exhausted and didn't want to do that. I was so frustrated with my symptoms and those negative tests that it occupied my entire thought process all day. Finally, walking out of work about 5 in the evening, I ran into a nurse friend who told me that if all I wanted was a lab test that I should make a telehealth appointment. I called urgent care and scheduled a virtual visit for 6pm.

I hadn't been tested in a week and half. While I waited for the visit, I decided to get a pregnancy test. I felt in my heart that I only needed one, but I knew if it was invalid, I'd be frustrated even more and the wait for Monday would be extremely long. I decided on two, just in case.

The telehealth provider ordered a confirmatory blood test and a urinalysis to make sure I didn't have a urinary tract infection that was causing my cramping in case my blood test was negative. I laughed to myself because I knew I didn't have a UTI as my breasts were also sore. But I did remember that a few weeks ago I started noticing my urine becoming more concentrated, having a darker color and a more pronounced urine smell. I agreed to the urinalysis just in case. If the blood test was negative, the telehealth provider would order a transvaginal ultrasound as a further work up of my symptoms.

We have our "midweek" service on Friday nights. I was purposefully there early and wanted to test before service started. In the bathroom, I read the directions of the test and prayed again in desperation. It was such a powerful prayer! I began speaking in tongues as I praised Him and thanked Him for His faithfulness to me. I poured out my frustrations with the symptoms I had and all the previous tests I had taken that were negative.

Following the instructions for the test, I started a three-minute timer on my phone. I sat the test beside my phone, stood up, buried my face against the bathroom stall and pleaded with Him. I was so frustrated thinking I was pregnant and seeing negative tests. I knew in my heart that I had to be pregnant and negative tests did not make sense.

"God, I *need* this test to be positive! Please!"

A short while later I wanted to look at the time, but didn't want to look at the test too early. I told myself I would just look at the timer quickly, then look away, hopefully not seeing the test in my peripheral vision. Knowing a negative test would be even more frustrating, I planned on waiting the full three minutes. However, the test was right beside my phone. It had been less than a minute and out of the corner of my eye I saw... TWO PINK LINES!

I felt numb.

I can't remember if I cried, screamed, or a little bit of both, but one thing was for sure: I was hysterical. I called Joey and told him to come immediately to the ladies bathroom. He came over by the water fountain right outside the door and I ran out screaming and crying, showing him the test, and asked him to tell me what it said. He looked at me and said, "I don't know."

To throw a little humor in what was such a joyfully tragic situation (if that makes any sense at all), the test - covered with my urine - was in my hand and I was pointing and waving it at him frantically. He looked at me calmly yet sternly and said, "get that thing away from me." In his defense, he was wearing a nice suit and tie. It was actually quite comical.

After a pause, his eyes never breaking contact with me, he said "I can't do this right now." His face was completely blank and expressionless. In a few moments, he needed to focus on the Word of the Lord as he spoke what God had given him for the congregation. This reality would take more than a few moments to process. It had been fourteen years!

We were drawing attention to ourselves, and I didn't know if we should tell people or how I was supposed to act. He kept reminding me I needed to calm down. I didn't know how. I didn't know what to do.

Was this really happening?

It was really positive!?

It was right about the time for pre-service prayer to start. I returned to the bathroom to gain some composure. In the meantime, he went to find Mama Pat. He told where I was and asked her to tell me to calm down. The moment she came in, I pulled her into the stall with me and locked the door behind her. I held up the test and asked, "what does it say?" I was still shocked and felt like I was in a dream. She smiled, shook her head as if to say, "I told you so" and said, "you're pregnant." She didn't seem surprised one bit. Praise God for saints of God who have unfailing faith!

The term "ugly cry" is the only way to describe the emotional response I had to this moment in my life. I ugly cried. There was nothing cute about any of the crying I did. My response was tragic, and I'm not sure why I responded that way. These weren't happy joyful tears. It was more than fourteen years of pent-up emotion, pain, and frustration. I kept looking at the test in disbelief. I actually had a positive test! Prayer had already begun at this point, and I wasn't sure I could keep my composure in the sanctuary.

I wasn't sure if Joey would want to tell anyone, but I wanted to tell Sis. Dartt, one of my dear friends in the Lord, a prayer warrior and a woman of God that I admire so much. I found her in a classroom preparing for children's church and showed her the test. We praised God together with laughter, dancing, and tears! Once it finally sank in that this was real, I sat smiling that entire service, my heart beaming with joy. I praised the Lord so much! I kept looking at her sitting across from me and she kept smiling as well. We were rejoicing! The Lord performed a miracle! After service, her husband told me that the Lord told him earlier in prayer that I was pregnant. God truly was doing a new thing!

And blessed is she that believed: for there shall be a performance of those things which were told her from the Lord."

Luke 1:45

15

On the Other Side of Surrender

I was on a spiritual high and there was nothing that could have brought me low – or so I thought.

We told everyone who would listen. We called his mom and sisters. We called my mom on video chat with my dad and brother present to show them the test as a surprise. I told the ladies who work in my office and those I came in contact with each day. I couldn't help but to give Him glory for what He had done. The week following I completely picked out all of the items on my baby registry and was ready to distribute the link. I thought it would give people plenty of time to purchase things on the list, and we could start buying the big things like the crib, car seat, etc. After all, this pregnancy was invincible! Why wait? But, I felt a hesitancy in my spirit like God was indeed telling me to wait, so I was obedient.

Joey was so supportive. He was gentle, loving, and considerate. One day, he asked "What do you think about the name Jonathan? It means gift from God." He searched for diaper bags and baby items on Amazon. He announced it at work. We work for the same hospital system, and his colleagues would congratulate me in the hallway as they passed by. It warmed my heart that he was talking about it. He was very nervous about mentioning it at first. It was such a shock to us both that this was reality.

Based on my symptoms, I estimated I was about five weeks pregnant. I assumed those early symptoms were ovulation symptoms and that I probably conceived mid to late February, with my first actual pregnancy symptoms starting just before Ministers Retreat. It was possible that those early symptoms were also pregnancy related, and I was getting false negatives. My mother reassured me that this happened to her the first several months of her pregnancy with me. I called an OB and scheduled an appointment for an ultrasound to confirm it was an intrauterine pregnancy and to check for a heartbeat.

The week before that appointment, I started having some spotting. I was told some of this could be expected and could be normal. Again, I truly felt this pregnancy was invincible. God had done a miracle and there was no way He was going to let anything happen to this pregnancy. I had confidence that He would not do that to me. He knows how difficult that would be and how long I've waited for this. I prayed and He answered. He is faithful and trustworthy.

While all of those things about the Lord are true, my spotting continued. I decided to schedule an earlier appointment just for peace of mind. My appointment was with a different OB, and it was a horrible experience. The only thing she could see was a gestational sac and a white area that she said "could be" the yolk sac starting to form. I measured five weeks and one day. Based on my calculations, at the time of this visit I expected to have been almost seven weeks or more. She kept prefacing everything she said with "if this is a viable pregnancy," words that tore through my heart like daggers.

If.

There was no confidence in that word.

The provider ordered a pregnancy hormone level. The test that was ordered by the Urgent Care provider was just a confirmatory positive or negative blood test. I went home from that appointment and went straight to bed. I was emotionally, physically, and spiritually drained.

Soon after, the brownish colored spotting turned to a bright red color. Each time I felt anxiety or worry start to creep up inside me, I'd run to my prayer room and cry out to God. Like Hannah, before I was even pregnant, I prayed that if God would grant me a son, I would dedicate him to Him and bring him up in a godly way. Once I found out I was pregnant, I praised God and told Him that I surrendered this child to Him, and like Manoah's wife, I prayed for God to show me how to bring him up in a godly way so that he would never depart from truth. Once again, I found myself before the altar crying out to God and surrendering this child to Him. Like the Shunamite woman embracing her promise whose very life was being threatened, I waited moment after moment not knowing what the outcome would be.

The words of Job kept running through my head, "Though He slay me, yet will I trust in Him" (Job 13:15). The three Hebrew boys, Shadrach, Meshach, and Abednego told the king that God had the power to deliver them out of the fiery furnace, but even if He didn't they would still not bow to serve any other God (Daniel 3:16-18). David fasted while his child was ill, waiting to see if the Lord really would allow his child to die (I1 Samuel 12:15-18). I knew God was in control and He could intervene. I just didn't know if He would.

As I sat there, I came to the realization that I could choose to be bitter with Him. I could choose right there in that moment to walk away from Him. I could even find excuses in those circumstances to justify my decision in doing so. But what about the other areas of my life that God had redeemed? All the countless other times He had provided and shown Himself faithful? The other miracles He had done for me?

I cried out, telling Him that I knew He could save this baby, but even if He didn't, I would continue to serve Him. As gut wrenching as it was to admit that I may have to come to terms with this if it was His plan, I knew it was true. I would continue living for Him and that would include praising Him, talking of His goodness. David, when trying to purchase property to build an altar of repentance after a decision he made that was outside of God's plan, was adamant that he was not going to sacrifice something to his God that did not cost him something. Up until this point, I was willing to sacrifice anything for the sake of His kingdom and to align myself with His will, but I never thought my walk with God would cost me this.

Something shifted inside of me.

I had been extremely blessed living for the Lord. He had always shown Himself faithful and it was easy for me to live for Him. But in my heart at this moment, I felt almost like He failed me, like He had forsaken me. Those thoughts were completely contrary to the Word of God. The enemy used my moments of weakness, trying to get me to turn my back on Him. I had to *choose*, no matter what it felt like, to serve God and to praise Him. He had still done a miracle. He was speaking with me and confirming this pregnancy along the way.

This was His will.

Regardless of the outcome of this pregnancy, it was still a miracle, and He still deserved praise! After over fourteen years of failed attempts, multiple doctor reports and tests that showed that my body was incapable of conceiving on its own, I became pregnant. I had no menstrual cycle for over 13 months prior to conception and was not currently doing anything to try to conceive other than my fasting and praying in January.

On Thursday, March 23, I got some repeat blood work drawn to see where my levels were after the bloodwork from the OB two days prior. I didn't have my results yet, but the bleeding increased when I stood. I had gone to work and before I was there even a half an hour, my bleeding worsened. I called Joey and had him pray with me, and then went home. It was better when I laid down, so I decided to take the day off and rest in bed. I no longer felt pregnant. I lost that spiritual connection I had with my baby. Most of my pregnancy symptoms started to fade. I felt worry and fear grip my heart. Joey kept assuring me everything would be okay, and that I shouldn't worry. He was so confident.

Looking back on this, it kills me that he was wrong. It hurts me to know that he allowed himself to open his heart up in a vulnerable way and it was broken. When we found out, he seemed apprehensive about sharing the news, but I was so confident of a positive outcome that I couldn't keep it secret. I felt guilty and somewhat responsible for his pain. I felt the symptoms that proved that there was a life growing inside of me. But this was his baby, too, and he didn't have what I had. Infertility, miscarriage, and loss affect every person in the relationship. When a husband and wife are joined together under God in the covenant of marriage, they become one flesh; what affects one affects the other. His pain was my pain, and I didn't know what to do with it. I didn't know what to do with my own pain.

I noticed the bleeding had worsened when I got out of bed the next day. I called the OB office and let them know what was happening. The nurse got the results from my labs the day before and the OB called me back to confirm that my greatest fears. I was miscarrying. The pregnancy hormone levels dropped when they should have doubled in number.

They told me to come in for an ultrasound and to speak with the physician assistant who specializes in infertility and miscarriage. I didn't have an ultrasound at that appointment, but she wanted me to come back the following week for an ultrasound to see if there was any tissue left in my uterus.

Tissue. That's all my baby was to them now. I hated this.

That entire weekend, I secretly prayed that God would redeem the situation and there would be a live thriving fetus in my womb at that ultrasound. I got lost in the internet reading accounts of women who had been diagnosed with an early loss and even had a dip in the pregnancy hormone. In these accounts, the pregnancy hormones began to increase again as they normally would and the follow-up ultrasound showed a living baby. These mothers unknowingly expected twins and while they did lose one, the other survived.

Although I knew nothing was impossible with my God, I also prepared my heart for what would come if He chose not to intervene. The world had pronounced my promise dead, but God had the final say, and I would need to be content with whatever He chose. Unfortunately, the ultrasound showed that my miscarriage was complete.

For several weeks I struggled with this. I knew it was an act of God and I didn't understand why He could allow this to happen when I trusted Him without any doubt in my heart. My faith was as pure as it had ever been. Nights were extremely hard. While I was pregnant, I would spend my nights battling insomnia by adding baby items to my registry, reading about how big my baby was, or watching birth vlogs and planning the details of my delivery. Now, all I had was this empty void. It was even more empty than barrenness. I felt as if I had nothing more to look forward to. At least before this I looked forward to the day I would find out I was pregnant. Now what? Life seemed to continue for everyone around me, but for me it came to a screeching halt. I didn't know what to do with this grief that I felt.

I didn't know how to feel about God or my knowledge of Him. I trusted Him, and from where I was standing, it looked like He let me down. I came to the realization that I trusted Him to do what I wanted Him to do and to do it my way. But He never once promised that. I realized that

I cannot have my way and His Will at the same time. You see, when we completely surrender something to Him, we surrender all the details, all the decision making, all of our wants and desires. We release all control and basically tell God "I don't want to have any say in the matter whatsoever because I know Your plans are better than mine." We release all expectations and submit to be content with the outcome.

It sounds good to *say* we surrender.

I believe we have good intentions to surrender when we say we are, but are we truly surrendering it all to Him?

I'm thankful that several of the ladies from my church family who are really close friends of mine took time out of their day to spend some time with my husband and me in our home during those initial days. But as time went on, I was left alone with this feeling inside of my heart that only God could mend, and it was a few weeks before I was ready to allow myself to be vulnerable enough to pray, "Lord, Your will be done."

One night, I was up crying and all I wanted was someone to call and share space with me as I cried. I couldn't utter words because I didn't know what to say. I sat in bed and cried and stared off to space, completely aghast. I texted a few ladies who were close to me and were lifting us up in prayer. No one knew what to say. They'd simply say, "I'm praying." There were no words, and I knew they felt my pain. This was a shock to everyone, and no one understood how this was His plan. Honestly, nothing anyone would have said in those dark, agonizing moments would have made any difference. There was a void so deep that only God could fill.

One friend who is spiritually sensitive told me she had sensed in the spirit that someone was experiencing deep emotional pain. I told her that was exactly how I felt. Those three words explained it perfectly: deep emotional pain.

A few weeks later, we had game night with that same friend and a few others. She told me later that night that She sensed that same feeling as soon as we walked through the door that night. She couldn't tell if it was my husband who walked in a few moments before me or if it were me. She prayed during our gathering that the Lord would make a way for her to be alone with us to talk. We ended up being the last ones to leave. She said the Lord told her that this was my "I see men walking as trees" moment, and that God was not finished yet. It became a comfort to me that God still had a plan and a promise for me.

She was referencing the book of Matthew which gives an account of Jesus' interaction with a certain blind man. After He led the man out of the city, He spit on his blind eyes, laid His lands on him, and asked him what he saw. The man looked up and said, "I see men as trees, walking" (Mark 6:24). Jesus put His hands upon the man's eyes once again, and when the man looked upward once more, he could see clearly. I don't know why God allowed this to happen, but one thing is for sure: He is not finished with me yet. Right now, my vision is blurry but there will be a day that I will see clearly. My story is still being written, and so is yours! More importantly, He is worthy of our praise!

This took my praise and worship to a deeper level. It's easy to praise Him when times are good and the waters of life are calm. But when your path seems uncertain, and the storms of this life are howling all around you, these times of desperate need are the times when we should reach into the depths of our spirit and exercise our trust and confidence in the One who goes before us by shouting with a voice of triumph, knowing the battle has already been won. The walls of Jericho shall fall. God has already given you the victory.

"Trust in the Lord with all thine heart; and lean not unto thine own understanding. In all thy ways acknowledge him, and he shall direct thy paths"

Proverbs 3:5-6

16

A Place of Rest and Safety

Before the start of 2023, the Lord began to speak the word "abide" into my spirit. I noticed it in scripture upon scripture that kept popping up in my day. I have a clear memory verse box that sits upon my desk at work that was a gift from a friend who invited me into the church when I was a new convert. Every few days, if not daily, my verse of the day would remind me of this word.

In most biblical occurrences of the original text, both Hebrew and Greek, this word means to tarry, dwell, or cleave to. While more modern translations of this verb agree with these definitions, this word can also be used to admonish rest or to remain in a state of constancy. This verb also commands the recipient of the word to endure, bear patiently, prepare, or to be prepared.

David cried out to God in Psalm 61:4, "I will abide in thy tabernacle for ever: I will trust in the covert of thy wings. Selah."

Selah.

Once again: pause and reflect on this statement.

During this psalm, David declared His comfort and trust in the Lord his God, who had been a place of shelter and a refuge from anything that was warring against him (Psalm. 61:3) He declares, "from the end of the earth will I cry unto thee, when my heart is overwhelmed: lead me to the rock that is higher than I. For thou, O God, hast heard my vows" (Psalm 61:2, 5). No matter the forces weighing against us, we have a Refuge, a place where we can run to and be safe (Proverbs 18:10).

I had a revelation not long ago about the current state of the world, and I truly feel led to mention it here. Our reactions to the storms of this life are dependent upon our view of the Master of those storms. It's inevitable that circumstances arise where we find ourselves on a ship in the midst of tempestuous waves and roaring winds tossing us to and fro. How we respond to those circumstances depends on our perception. Are we in the boat alone with the Lord seemingly nowhere in sight? Are we in the boat with our eyes on the Lord who we recognize as our refuge only after trying to bear it in our own strength? Or do we find ourselves in the boat knowing that He is in our midst and calling upon Him because we realize that left to our own devices, we cannot make it through?

The book of Matthew gives accounts of storms the disciples encountered and how they reacted to those storms depending on where Jesus was in their midst. In Matthew 8, Jesus called His disciples to follow Him, to which they were readily obedient. Somewhere along their journey across the sea, they found themselves in a violent storm. Immediately, they ran to wake Him, declaring, "save us: we perish" (Matthew 8:25). They knew His capabilities because of the close relationship they forged with Him. Although they felt threatened and intimidated by the storm, they ultimately knew that He could, and would, save them.

In chapter 14, the disciples find themselves in the midst of the sea once again. This time, Jesus sent them out on their own. Again, a storm arose that became more than they could bear in their own strength. Imagine how they must have felt. They knew they had a Savior, but He was seemingly nowhere in sight. As they battled the waves, tormented and distressed, Jesus walked toward them upon the water. The storm that raged all around them was beneath His feet – a powerful depiction of His divine authority and power (1 Corinthians 15:24-28). Mark's account of this event states that Jesus would have passed them by (Mark 6:48). Significantly, it was the fourth, or last, watch of the night, indicating that He allowed them to endure the storm for quite a while as a trial of their faith. He tested them to see if they would call upon Him in their greatest time of need, when it seemed the situation was beyond His reach or when they were seemingly alone in their circumstances.

When they finally noticed a figure walking on the water, they cried out in fear thinking it was a ghost. Fear, instead of faith, was their initial reaction to the unknown. They didn't recognize their Savior walking toward them amid the storm, but when it seemed time was running out, He was there . . . just in time.

I'm thankful for the mercy of our God! Without delay, He spoke a word of peace, "Be of good cheer; it is I; be not afraid" (Matthew 14:29). Peter cried out to Him, "Lord, if it's really you, call me to a place where I too can be treading peacefully upon the waves that threaten to overtake me." Have you ever prayed, 'God, use me?' or 'Lord, increase my faith so that I trust more in You?' Bro. Lee Stoneking frequently admonishes believers to be careful what they ask for, knowing that God is faithful to answer. If we pray to be used, we may end up actually feeling used! In other words, if you lack faith, He will put you in situations to build your faith. If you lack patience, you can rest assured that your patience will be tried. It's the same way with trust. If we trust, there's no place for fear.

In His true nature, He answered that prayer immediately and Peter stepped out in faith upon the waters, his eyes focused on the God whose power was exalted high above the power of any storm that would attempt to sway him.

But something happened.

Peter took his eyes off Jesus and once again focused on the storms that raged all around him. He chose fear over faith. Remember what Bro. Hernandez said? Faith and fear cannot coincide. It's one or the other. Peter was literally drowning in fear. Once again, the hand of Jesus was there to lift him out of his circumstances. What a faithful God we serve!

I was visiting home not long before writing this and attended a small church plant that just celebrated five years being in the community. Sis. Olsen, the pastor's wife, spoke a word of encouragement behind the pulpit. It was such a timely message and of great encouragement to me. God gave her a revelation about Jesus' response to Peter's fear. She asked Him, "Lord, how could you say Peter had little faith? He walked upon the water." His response to her was that while his faith was great to begin with, it was not sustained. It was short lived. How often do we see our faith rise when we see the hand of God in our situation, but as time goes on, we become once again distracted by what our natural eyes see instead of what He tells us in His Word?

This was definitely the case in my walk with God, specifically related to infertility. I knew what His Word said. I knew with certainty He had spoken a word of promise and had confirmed it on multiple occasions. I didn't feel led to pursue any additional medical intervention, despite my desperate desire to do whatever I could.

I stumbled upon some adoption vlogs where couples videoed their experience from the time they decided on adoption, the steps they took to pursue it, the call declaring they had been chosen, and their initial moments uniting with the child they adopted. I felt an aching in my heart, an unease or state of unrest. It was as if some part of me knew I would not feel that connection with a child the way I longed for. It wasn't the response I had when I watched birth vlogs of women holding the baby, they conceived and labored. It was a feeling of detachment and sorrow instead of hope and anticipation. To me, it felt like this would be another "Hagar" situation. "*It may be* adoption" wasn't even a thought in my mind at this point. I knew this wasn't in His plan.

Similarly, when I heard success stories of women who endured infertility and had success with IVF or other medical interventions, it left me feeling empty. I didn't want to be pressured to succumb to those other options. My desire was to conceive unknowingly, experience the joy of finding out I was pregnant, contemplate sweet ways to notify my husband and our family, experience all that pregnancy had to offer, the highs and the lows, and then experience the rawness of a natural unmedicated birth. I wanted my body to function in the way God designed.

Time and time again, He spoke peace and promise. Time and time again, I'd ride the high tides of faith that was unshakeable and unwavering *until* time and distance from that spoken word caused my faith to dwindle. Time and time again, I'd find myself back in a desperate place, completely overwhelmed with my situation, crying out to God wondering where He was in my pain. All along, He was beckoning me to a deeper place, a place where no matter what it seemed like with my natural senses, that I could rest in Him – abide in Him.

It wasn't until I contemplated the closing of this book that I realized God had been calling me to abide in Him before this year began. It has been a year full of seemingly endless trials. He was preparing me, calling me to a place of refuge and safety so that I didn't have to experience the unnecessary distress that these circumstances would provide. He saw the storms ahead: overwhelming responsibilities at work that would dare to diminish my peace and joy, a miscarriage that would reveal how unshakeable my faith truly was, the loss of a dog that I mothered for almost fourteen years as if it was our first child, walking with my father as he suffered a massive heart attack and deteriorating health that threatened his life more than once. He was aware that I would witness the burnout and exhaustion my mother experienced daily as she tried to work and care for five people, including two grandchildren aged six and ten, while still trying to provide meals and keep up with the demands of keeping a home. All of this was of course in addition to all the other stressors life brings our way.

The accumulation of this stress was unbearable. It was a heavy weight that quickly became too much for me to carry. I thought I was managing it, but over time I was spending less time in prayer and less time reading my Bible. Although I continued to pray morning and evening, and read my Bible every day, those prayer times were quick and shallow. I was lucky if I read more than a chapter or two most days. It was not the prayer life and the devotion I once had nor was it what I wanted. I could feel the Lord drawing me. I'd feel guilty and would attempt to catch up on my reading by listening to my Bible while I was driving or doing chores around the house. Occasionally, while I was checking a box with my Bible reading and going through the motions of my Christian walk, something would stand out to grab my attention, but more often than not I couldn't tell you what I had just listened to or read.

I'd pour myself out to him at church and in corporate prayer times that would force me to stop, slow down, and give me an opportunity to get into His presence. During corporate times of worship or prayer, I'd get frustrated because I really just wanted to be alone with the Lord.

I was distracted.

I was completely overwhelmed with my eyes on my circumstances, and not on Jesus. I had allowed the main thing to take second place, or third place, or worse. This continued for a little over a year until I reached a point where I could not eat. Anxiety and stress had far exceeded my limits and all of the muscles in my neck, shoulders, and face were so tense that I literally could not swallow. If I attempted to eat something, it would get stuck. It reached a point where I couldn't even eat the gelatin that I mushed up in my mouth. The muscles were so tense that even the feeling of anything in my esophagus made me feel like I could not breathe. This left me with incredible fear to attempt to eat anything. After several days of only liquids and protein shakes, I heard His voice speaking that single word once again. Abide. He reminded me that He had a place of refuge for me all along.

He has never promised that we would not endure pain or distress in this life. He does promise, however, that He will never leave us or forsake us. He promises to be with us in the midst of the battles we face, going before us and fighting for our victory. His Word assures us that the things we face, although painful and burdensome, He can use for our good. If there was no heat or pressure, we would not change.

We often want to run from the fiery trials of this life. Once upon a time, I wished I didn't have to go through infertility. It's incredibly hard! However, this journey has solidified who I am in Him, caused me to rely on Him when I had no strength, shown me that I can experience joy in the midst of sorrow and pain, and that He is my fortress that I can run into and feel safe. A place where I can abide in the fire instead of running from it, knowing that in the fire He is refining me, clearing the impurities within me so that I reflect more and more of His image.

He is pursuing each of us, calling us to abide in Him. He wants us to trust in His nature, knowing that He will not break His promises, nor will He go back on the words that He had spoken (Psalm 89:34). Even when we fail Him, He will never fail us (Psalm 89:31, 33). He is faithful and trustworthy. When the road ahead gets rough and seems too hard to bear, He calls us to a deep place in Him where we can feel secure.

When we look at all of the barren women recorded in scripture who focused their vision on the Lord, we see that their burdens did not go unfruitful. Their long-suffering and forbearing resulted in blessings beyond measure. Their testimonies serve as an encouragement to each and every one of us who walks a similar path. More importantly, they bear witness to the King of Kings and show forth His glory.

Peter, who denied Jesus on more than one occasion despite promising the Lord that he would never, whose faith was replaced by fear despite all that Jesus had allowed him to witness, was the rock on which He chose to build His church (Matthew 16:18).

Jesus Himself willingly endured the most excruciating trials, including the cross. He was grieved and distressed so deeply that He sweat blood. This has only been recorded in a small number of cases throughout history and is caused by an extreme level of stress. No matter the agony the trials I have faced have caused me to endure, I have never been stressed that much! He has compassion for us when we are hurting; He knows pain in a way that, thankfully, not many if any of us will ever experience.

I don't know what lies ahead of you in the journey that you're facing. I don't know what the Lord has spoken into your heart. But I do know one thing, He is for you. He has a plan and a purpose for your pain. He is calling you to abide in Him, in the secret place, the dwelling of the most High (Psalm 91:1), that innermost place not many visit despite the constant invitations to enter in, the Holy of Holies. It does not come without an altar, a sacrifice, or surrender. Only when we *choose* to let go of the reins, to stop resisting the flames, and purpose our heart to say, "Thy Will be done," do we find freedom from these burdens.

Psalm 91 declares that if we dwell in this secret place, a place of surrender and trust, He will be our shelter, our covering, and our deliverer, and the things that move the rest of the world, will not move us. "For I the LORD thy God will hold thy right hand, saying unto thee, Fear not; I will help thee" (Isaiah 41:13). "Because he hath set his love upon me, therefore will I deliver him: I will set him on high, because he hath known my name. He shall call upon me, and I will answer him. I will be with him in trouble: I will deliver him, and honour him" (Psalm 91:14-15).

I can feel the unconditional, sacrificial, and voluntary love of God in these statements. Whether He calls the storms of our lives to be still or He leads us out onto the waters, there's one certainty: He is still God in the storm. (Mark 4:41, Matthew 8:27).

"Come and hear, all ye that fear God, and I will declare what he hath done for my soul."

Psalm 66:16

17

My Heart Doth Magnify the Lord

Dear reader, it is my prayer that the contents of this book you have paged through have ignited a flame inside of your heart that bursts with anticipation of the plans He has for you! I pray that you have found encouragement enough to stand and wait on the Lord.

There's an urgency in my spirit to introduce you to yet another woman who was labeled barren. Her name is Elisabeth, and her story can be found in the first chapter of Luke. In the middle of a prayer meeting, the angel Gabriel appeared to her husband Zacharias and informed him that his prayer had been heard. His wife, who was called barren, would conceive a son. Not just any son, but a son to be mightily used by God, consecrated and filled with the Holy Ghost from the womb, a man who shall bear the testimony of the Lord and turn other's hearts toward Him. His birth would be a time of gladness and rejoicing – well worth the wait they had endured (Luke 1:9-17).

When he heard of this promise, Zacharias asked what sign he could expect to confirm this promise. It's been a long time in this season, and although he knew his God was able, it was a little difficult to believe. The response was this: "The words will be fulfilled in their season" (Luke 1:30).

Scripture assures us that there's a season for everything (Ecclesiastes 3:1-10) and that "He hath made everything beautiful in His time" (Ecclesiastes 3:11). When the time was right, Elisabeth would conceive, and she did – according to His Word.

Shortly after, her cousin Mary also conceived, and the two joined together in a powerful time of praise and worship. They were truly honored to be a vessel God could use as He saw fit. Elisabeth spoke enthusiastically, "Blessed is she that believed: for there shall be a performance of those things which were told her from the Lord" (Luke 1:45). Mary cried out in adoration for her God and the mighty things He had done, "My heart doth magnify the Lord, and my spirit hath rejoiced in God my Savior" (Luke 1:46-47, see also Luke 1:48-55)

My heart doth magnify the Lord! What an incredible feeling of overwhelming joy!

Seasons come and go.

This season will end.

"Weeping may endure for a night, but joy cometh in the morning" (Psalm 30:5). While now may feel like a time of enduring, abide in Him. Soon there will be a time of rejoicing. It is my prayer that you find peace in this season and that your fruitfulness bears a testimony of just how great of a God we serve! All for His glory!

"And I said, This is my infirmity: but I will remember the years of the right hand of the most High. I will remember the works of the Lord: surely I will remember thy wonders of old. I will meditate also of all thy work, and talk of thy doings. Thy way, O God, is in the sanctuary: who is so great a God as our God?"

Psalm 77:10-13

Selah.

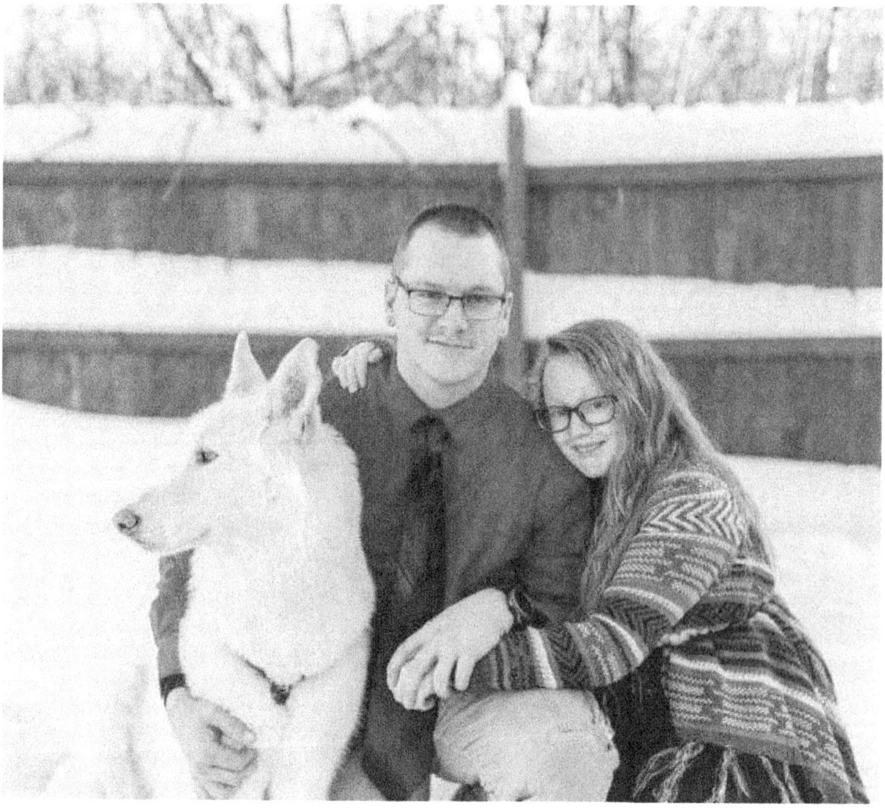

About the Authors

Crystal Essex is a Registered Nurse (R.N.) and, along with her husband Joey, pastors the Sitka United Pentecostal Church in Sitka, Alaska. Their love for outdoor adventures – kayaking, riding ATVs in the bush, skiing, snow machining, hiking, and capturing moments through photography – mirrors their journey of faith: expansive, challenging, and filled with beauty. Crystal and Joey share their home with three dogs, Lilly, Aurora, and Denali, which bring joy and companionship to their adventurous lives.

Fruitful is more than a book; it's an invitation to find strength and solace in God's promises, making it an invaluable resource for anyone facing the pain of infertility and loss while holding onto faith for a fruitful outcome.

Made in the USA
Columbia, SC
14 June 2024